PITCHING SECRETS OF THE PROS

Big-League Hurlers Reveal the Tricks of Their Trade

WAYNE STEWART

New York   Chicago   San Francisco   Lisbon   London   Madrid   Mexico City
Milan   New Delhi   San Juan   Seoul   Singapore   Sydney   Toronto

1 2 3 4 5 6 7 8 9 0   AGM/AGM   3 2 1 0 9 8 7 6 5 4

ISBN 0-07-141825-3

McGraw-Hill books are available at special quantity discounts to use as premiums and sales promotions, or for use in corporate training programs. For more information, please write to the Director of Special Sales, Professional Publishing, McGraw-Hill, Two Penn Plaza, New York, NY 10121-2298. Or contact your local bookstore.

This book is printed on acid-free paper.

To my wife, Nancy, and my sons, Sean and Scott

Also by Wayne Stewart
Baseball Bafflers
Baseball Oddities
Baseball Puzzlers
Fathers, Sons & Baseball
The History of the Anaheim Angels
The History of the Atlanta Braves
The History of the Chicago White Sox
The History of the Cincinnati Reds
The History of the Cleveland Indians
The History of the Colorado Rockies
The History of the Detroit Tigers
The History of the Kansas City Royals
The History of the Los Angeles Dodgers
The History of the Pittsburgh Pirates
Hitting Secrets of the Pros
Indians on the Game

Contents

Acknowledgments

FIRST AND FOREMOST, thanks to my editor, Mark Weinstein, who once again came up with a great idea. This time it was for a series of books on inside tips and information straight from the source—big-league players, coaches, and managers. The two books thus far are on hitting secrets and on pitching insights. Clearly, without him these books would never have come to fruition.

Second, it was great talking baseball and working with editorial team leader Craig Bolt. It really helps to work with folks who know publishing as well as baseball, and that's been the case with Mark and now Craig.

Finally, a big thanks to the pros themselves, especially those who went way beyond merely giving me a few quick answers to my queries: Ken Griffey Sr. and Jr., Rudy Jaramillo, Ryan Klesko, Lee Smith, Trevor Hoffman, Merv Rettenmund, Billy Wagner, Jeff Bagwell, Craig Biggio, Johnny Damon, Scott Stewart, Jim Thome, Willie Upshaw, Eric Byrnes (and his father, Jim), Terry Francona, Rickey Henderson, Luis Gonzalez, Kent Tekulve, Duane Espy, Tom McCraw, Dr. Charles Maher of the Indians; along with the media departments of many clubs, especially the Cleveland Indians, the San Francisco Giants (particularly Bobby Evans), the Anaheim Angels, and the Arizona Diamondbacks (with a special thanks to Susan Webner).

Also, a special thanks to Gray & Co. for giving me permission to use material from *Indians on the Game*, a book that I did for them a few years back.

Foreword

ONE OF THE THINGS that drives me nuts is when a guy will say, "This guy is a good fastball hitter." Well, who's *not*? If you can't hit the fastball, you've got no chance. I said, "If I'm a good fastball pitcher, does that mean I'm not going to throw him a fastball?" You have to make quality pitches.

The only secrets to my success were just going out there every day and taking one game at a time. Also, I always liked to know that my teammates were depending on me in tough situations. "Smitty's coming in, we got the game." That was the main thing I loved about pitching. And if you can see that with your fielders, when you go out there, that's great. When you go out there and it's ball one, ball two, you've got your fielders on their heels.

When I came out there, I was deliberate to the plate, but my guys behind me knew that I was going to throw strikes, that they had to be alert. Even when I struck out guys, they were still thinking, "Hey, Smitty's going to throw strikes to this guy. Is he going to hit the ball? Maybe."

The thing about being around the plate is you start getting respect from the umpires to the point where you can come off the plate a little more and still get strikes called. When I got to the point where I could throw all of my pitches for strikes, and at *any* count, I became a better pitcher.

Early in my career, I was a thrower. Then I learned the hitters. I mean, I watched extra batting practice. I think that was the main thing that helped me out so much in my career. I worked and watched the other team. The guys asked, "Why are you watching these guys hit?" I said, "I'm watching because a hitter, if he has any shortcomings, he's going to work on it in batting practice. That's why they call it batting *practice*. If there's a ball that he can't hit and things that he wants to work on hitting that ball, he's going to work on it there."

The extra men that I knew I was going to face late in the game, the pinch hitters, I watched those guys. I'd sit in the dugout pregame, and if it was a team on which I knew some of the guys, I'd go out there and stand around the cage with them—but I was watching the hitters.

And another thing I did, I watched the umpires. You know, you heard that old thing about Smitty being in the clubhouse asleep during the game? You don't get eighteen years in the big leagues sleeping. I watched the umpires and how their strike zones fluctuated and how they called the ball in or out.

And I found out throughout my career that they would ring a guy up on a third strike with a ball going away, more so than they will inside. For some reason, the umpire sees that ball away from the hitter better. If you threw a ball inside and the batter is throwing his arms all over the place, I think the umpires watch that.

It depends on the hitter and the umpire, but I knew the umpires who would call pitches down and who called the ball up. I knew the guys by their first names and when I'd walk out there, I'd greet them—"Hey, Eric, how ya doing?"—because that borderline pitch means a lot.

I watched them from the monitor in the clubhouse. I could see if they were calling the ball off the plate, if they were calling the ball inside, up, or down.

I also loved being out there in what all the people thought was a pressure situation—I was comfortable. When I was out there, I was never nervous. I was nervous sitting on the bench watching my other guys play. I'd be pulling for them, but I would be nervous.

Now I'm coaching for the Giants and I am nervous for the *whole* game, watching the kids play. When I went between the lines I was comfortable with everything. Of course, when I was young, I didn't even like being a relief pitcher!

Now I like working with the young pitchers. We have some really good pitchers, and I like working with the kids, because hopefully I can keep some of them from making some mistakes that I made between the lines.

The toughest thing in this world to do, in any sport, I think, is to hit a baseball, a round ball with a bat. And the best hitter is a loser 70 percent of the time. There's no other job where you can be a loser 70 percent of the time and be the best at what you do. So I figure, 70 [outs] out of 100 at-bats? My chances are pretty good at getting some outs. I cannot get them if I walk him. If I get behind, his percentages are going to go up, but a guy can hit a bullet off of me and still make an out. And if the best guy is only going to get 30 hits out of 100 at-bats, then the rest of the guys are not that good. As a coach, I want my pitchers to realize that.

I think what separates a good pitcher from a great one is work ethics and heart. I've seen so many guys that had the talent to be great pitchers, but they didn't work at it.

You know that little extra that you put into it? Some guys are told, "You've got to run 15 liners," running in the outfield, foul pole to foul pole, and the guy always runs exactly 15, doesn't do anything else to make himself better. He just does enough to get by.

A pitcher you want on the mound for the big game is a guy who has heart. He's a guy who's not afraid to lose. Most guys go out there and say, "Man, I hope I don't lose." You gotta take a chance of getting beat when you go out there. If you make good pitches consistently, that's going to be the toll for you. You make those quality pitches to hitters, and you're going to win.

—LEE SMITH
MAJOR LEAGUE BASEBALL'S ALL-TIME LEADER IN SAVES

1

Styles of Pitching

THINKING PITCHERS, OF course, are well aware of many different approaches to mound success. Hundreds of pitchers have become stars while employing diverse styles. Satchel Paige, for example, stressed the importance of control and of getting ahead of hitters. He simply said, "Just take the ball and throw it where you want to. Throw strikes. Home plate don't move."

The story goes that in 1948, when Bill Veeck was about to sign Paige as major league baseball's oldest rookie ever at 42, the 22-year veteran of the Negro League was given an impromptu tryout. Baseball lore has it they used a gum wrapper for a home plate and Paige hit that minuscule strike zone four of five times. When he passed his control test, Veeck signed him and Paige didn't disappoint. He sizzled, going 6–1, while holding opponents to a meager .087 batting average. He said of his accuracy, "It got so I could nip frosting off a cake with my fastball."

Norman Lumpkin, who also played in the Negro League, said he vividly remembers the legendary Paige and his style. "Early in his career, he'd spot his fastball as his only pitch," recalled Lumpkin, "but he'd hit spots. He threw the curve late in his career."

With Paige's pinpoint control, pitching was relatively easy. Lumpkin recalled, "When he was in a good mood he'd put on a show. He'd put down a handkerchief [as a makeshift home plate] and the catcher put out a target, and he'd hit it."

During a start in the 2000 season, Detroit's Brian Moehler's last six innings of his complete game victory over Baltimore featured outstanding control on his part. He threw just 10 pitches out of the strike zone. His accuracy dated back to his childhood. "My first catcher was my dad, who refused to wear pads," he began. "To avoid hurting my father, I learned to throw strikes. He used to catch me from when I was eight or nine years old up through college."

Sounds simple, but closer Matt Mantei knows otherwise. While a fan might feel pitchers should be able to throw strikes all day long with batting machine regularity, Mantei said with a chuckle, "I wish it was easy. I tell you what, if it was easy, everybody would be playing baseball.

"But you know what, I've watched games from the stands and it's like, 'This does seem easy.' But it's not. It's hard to throw a 95-, 96-mile-an-hour fastball where guys can't hit it; it's not just throwing a strike."

Jeff Nelson once told a story illustrating how it's so easy to give advice, but not so easy to execute it. He said one of his managers, Lou Piniella, had very little patience. Nelson told the *New York Times*, "He tells you, 'Throw the ball over the plate.' You feel like saying, 'Is that what I'm supposed to do? I didn't know that. I thought I was supposed to come out here and walk everybody.'"

Mantei said that if a pitcher didn't have to worry about trying to put the ball where it wouldn't get drilled, if he simply had to put the ball in the strike zone, then he could hit the catcher's mitt "probably nine out of ten or eight out of ten times. There's a lot of muscle memory involved and a lot of mechanics are involved in it—you just gotta get to that certain slot."

Clyde Wright, never a hard thrower, preaches a key lesson. "Throw the ball over the plate," he said emphatically, stressing control and avoiding free passes, which almost inevitably haunt pitchers. He tells young pitchers they should always remember that "only one guy can bat at a time, right? Doubleday gave you nine guys to fight that one. Let him hit it." When Wright threw a no-hitter in 1970, he whiffed but one batter.

Clyde preached about Hall of Famers such as Warren Spahn who didn't throw very hard, as well as "Bullet" Bob Gibson who didn't throw in the high 90s, yet posted a phenomenal 1.12 ERA in 1968. So, it's true that one can win without possessing super speed.

Cy Young Award winner Greg Maddux has a fastball that probably moves more than any active pitcher's, and he can make it sink or run to the inside or outside portion of the plate. Yet he feels his changeup is just as vital to his success because it keeps hitters' timing messed up.

Likewise, Cy Young, who gave his name to the pitchers' ultimate trophy, felt his ability to hit spots was his key to success. He went so far as to say, "Control is what kept me in the big leagues for 22 years."

According to *The Pitcher* by John Thorn and John Holway, in 1968, when Denny McLain won 31 games, he threw an incredible 95 percent of his pitches over for strikes. And Spahn was famous for throwing strikes while avoiding the heart of the plate, making his living working the black border of home plate. He said his spot was a minuscule 2½ inches on each corner. "I never use the rest [of the plate]," he proudly said.

Highly respected pitching coach Leo Mazzone of the Atlanta Braves chimed in, "That's the biggest problem you see among pitchers—they can't control their fastball. They're too busy trying to trick hitters." So the Braves pitchers under Mazzone's lead stress command of the fastball.

While control artists make up a definite slice of the pitching population, there are many other styles around. In May of 2003, Mark Mulder of the A's got off to a torrid 6–1 start. He said his success came from an aggressive approach. "I'm going to go after everybody. It's like, 'Here it is, put it in play.' I'm going to throw strikes and try to get quick outs."

Some pitchers feel they must come "right at" the batters, and not give in to them. Their approach is to attack the hitter regardless of the count, even if it means throwing a fastball in a situation where the hitter is looking fastball. Veteran pitcher Dennis Cook felt he had to pitch that way, unafraid to challenge hitters, rather than giving in and winding up walking a ton of them. He felt that if he did surrender a home run using his methods, at least it would be with nobody aboard.

He labeled himself a "location pitcher." "I throw fastballs, but I'm not overpowering by any means [he throws in the mid-80s]. I'm just a guy who has to hit my spots." Then he delved into his propensity for challenging hitters. "I don't like to give in to the batter, that's just my personality. I'm not a mechanics pitcher, either, I just pick it up and throw it."

Many pitchers and hitters will tell you that such thinking is all part of the game. Hitters say, "I respect a pitcher [like Cook] for coming at me with fastballs, not trying to play it cute," but you'd expect them to say that. Why would any pitcher take Cook's attitude?

Philosophies differ, of course, and many pitchers in the early 2000s didn't agree with Cook, avoiding pitching to and challenging sluggers, most notably Barry Bonds. In 2002, Bob Brenly, manager of the Arizona Diamondbacks, gave his view: "I think it'd all be dependent upon game situations—who the hitter is, what the score is. There are a lot of determining factors, but there are a lot of pitchers out there—we've got a couple on our own staff, who'd rather throw a fastball down the middle of the plate on a 3-1 count and force that guy [hitter] to put it in play than nibble around and maybe walk the guy and now you give up a two-run homer.

"Curt Schilling gives up his share of home runs, Rick Helling gives up a lot of homers, Brian Anderson is a guy who gives up a lot of home runs," he said, rattling off members of his staff, "but fortunately, they don't walk a lot of guys and most of the time they're solo home runs.

"We joke about the 'rally-killing solo home run,' the other team has no one on base and they have to start all over again. But I think there's something to be said for challenging hitters in those situations."

Pete Rose began a torrid hitting streak on June 14 of 1978, a skein that didn't end until August 1 after he had hit safely in 44 straight contests. In his final at-bat, the one that snapped his streak, he faced the sidearming Gene Garber of the Atlanta Braves. Garber, whose style was to finesse hitters at times, never challenged Rose. On a 2-2 Rose was thwarted when he foul tipped a changeup into the catcher's mitt for strike three.

In postgame interviews Rose expressed his disdain for Garber saying, "He pitched like it was the seventh game of the World Series. I had one pitch to swing at that was a strike. Most pitchers just challenge a guy in that situation." He felt Garber was also nibbling at the plate, forcing

Rose to chase something bad or, and this was unlikely with the streak on the line, settle for drawing a walk.

Garber countered by saying it was his job, his duty to get Rose, or for that matter, any batter out, and do so the best way he felt he could retire them. So, why challenge him? Why give him a fastball, a pitch Rose thrived on for decades? Rose wanted a mano a mano confrontation; Garber wanted to go with his out pitch. Garber went with it and won the battle. Later he commented, "He gets paid to get hits. I get paid to get outs."

Steve Reed, who throws a little bit like Garber (Reed's deliveries come from more down, submarine style), agrees with the former Braves pitcher, totally unconcerned about what hitters think. "I'm going to get you out any way that I think that I can get you out.

"Why would I have a macho thing trying to challenge you when I can get you out with a slider? You can scream at me all you want while you go sit down on the bench. He can say all he wants [complaining] while he's drinking his water. I'm not going to sit there and challenge you and then get beat with something that I think you can hit. That's stupidity."

Then there's a blend of caution and aggressiveness displayed by another Cy Young winner, Tom Glavine. He said that when he enters an inning in which a dangerous hitter is due up to the plate, he "bears down extra hard on the guys before him." His goal is to have the bases empty when he has to face such a star so that he can work him carefully, perhaps even walking him—which is a whole lot better than serving up a hittable pitch.

Some pitchers, dating back to men such as Dizzy Dean, pitched with this interesting and similar idea in mind: work extra hard at getting the weak sticks. If a pitcher can record what should be "automatic" outs, then when the .333 hitters get their inevitable share of hits, they won't hurt as much since they'll come, in theory, with empty bases.

Eight-time batting champ Tony Gwynn, who hardly ever changed his approach and stance at the plate, said that Glavine was just the opposite when they faced each other. The crafty Glavine would move his spot on the rubber and change his delivery to thwart Gwynn. Further, according to *Baseball Digest*, another wily pitcher, Orel Hershiser, tried to foil Gwynn by "never releasing a pitch from the same place twice."

Mazzone tries to keep his pitchers' strategies simple. He wrote: "I tell my pitchers to focus on being in command of the fastball, learn how to throw the down-and-away strike consistently, and change speeds to keep the hitters off balance."

He also said that while his pitchers certainly know that opposing hitters like to go after first-pitch fastballs, he doesn't care. He will still have his pitcher offer up fastballs to start hitters off. His logic is that if you can throw a fastball for a strike, aiming down and away, the pitcher will either get ahead in the count or get an out on one pitch—a very economical way to, say, begin an inning. Of course, the pitcher must have control and not groove a fat pitch.

In his book *Pitching*, Orioles standout Jim Palmer said that he threw the ball as if he was "trying to hand it to the catcher" because this helped him "drive off the mound" rather than having him try to reach out. He also used that style since it makes pitchers "throw not only with your arm but with your body as well." He felt that young pitchers who stand up straight and sort of "flip the ball" to the plate put strain on their shoulder and elbow.

Meanwhile, in yet another fine book, *Nolan Ryan's Pitcher's Bible*, the fireballing artist said he liked the "tall and fall" style of pitching over the "dip and drive" method. He defined tall and fall as "taking a controlled fall toward home plate in the tall posture you achieve at balance." Dipping and diving, he said, is "pushing off the rubber as you reach your balance, dipping down, and then releasing the baseball."

Ryan admitted the driving off method worked for Tom Seaver and Jerry Koosman, but agreed with Tom House about the importance of "tall and fall." House contended that as a pitcher ages it becomes difficult to push off and use the dip-and-dive method. Ryan added, "It requires a lot of physical strength and makes it tough to throw a curveball."

Yet another Cy Young Award recipient, Rick Sutcliffe, once said, "In the majors, the physical part of the game is over—it becomes mental. Baseball is a game of adjustments. Those who make adjustments are a success."

Smart pitchers, upon seeing a trend with a given hitter, might change their way of throwing to him. In 1999 Omar Vizquel hit a career high .333, hitting exactly .333 both righty and lefty. Finally, around mid-August of 2000, opposing pitchers felt that "enough was enough" and shut him down when he was hitting right-handed.

His manager, Charlie Manuel, spotted the adjustment pitchers had made. "Left-handers are keeping the ball away from Omar," Manuel stated. "They're throwing him changeups and taking the pop out of his bat. With the count 3-0, 3-1, 3-2, and the bases loaded, I've seen them throw Omar changeups and sliders. Usually you don't do that with a guy who's 5'7". Managers like Billy Martin and Ralph Houk are probably rolling over in their graves, but that's how the game has changed."

Manuel noted, "This whole game's about adjustments. We have advance scouting now, we have all kind of videotapes and rooms with satellite systems and it's all adjustments [based on knowledge gained]."

Former big-league reliever Dave Otto said another key is "to make adjustments within the game. It's important if you're struggling to be able to adjust." He added, "I think it's important just to get the hitter out, so you take it one pitch at a time. I think that relieves some of the pressure. You put other things out of your mind and concentrate on the pitch."

Sometimes a pitcher's offensive exploits actually hurt his pitching, causing him to lose his focus. Dennis Cook tells the tale. "I hit a home run versus Fernando Valenzuela, a three-run shot. I got around the bases real quick; I was pretty excited. I was so excited, I went out the next inning and got shelled. I went out thinking about the home run and not enough about pitching."

Some pitchers like to change their starting point on the rubber in order to make an adjustment, often moving only slightly to the left or right. While observing Arizona southpaw pitcher Eddie Oropesa work one random at-bat in 2003, it was noted that he began with his left heel barely making contact with the corner of the rubber on the first base side. A few pitches later, he shifted a good ten inches toward the third base side, in the more conventional location for his foot. He did that for just one pitch, returning to the original spot to finish out the hitter.

Interestingly, Lee Smith said he moved his location on the mound "only when there was a fast runner and I was going to throw to first. I would get on the first base side of the rubber." It was his way of stealing an inch or two on his pickoff throws in the sport known by cliché as being "a game of inches." Smith, well aware of how many bang-bang calls there are in baseball, said of the trite "inches" phrase, "Trust me, it is."

He never had the feeling that runners picked up on his telltale move. "I don't think so," he chuckled. "I wear a size 15 shoe, I don't think they could tell whether I was on the rubber or not." Again, working out of the stretch as a reliever, Smith refused to move over on the rubber in an effort to locate his pitches in or out.

One lasting adjustment stemmed from a rather unusual event. In the 1989 NLCS, Maddux and his catcher had a conference on the mound before facing Will Clark. Maddux whispered his strategy to his catcher. Shortly after that, Clark drilled a home run and later revealed he had read Maddux's lips. When the then-Cubs pitcher learned this, he changed his ways—from that moment on whenever he discusses strategy, he covers his mouth with his glove.

As a matter of fact, he not only disguises what he says on the mound, he is discreet off the mound, too. He and controversy are poles apart. "I'm not going to do anything or say anything that makes a hitter remember me," he declared.

Pitchers "mess around" with the baseball in order to get it to move in various ways and directions. Cameron Cairncross, who once pitched for Cleveland, said a pitcher will explore different ways to hold the ball with the seams. "If you're looking for a two-seam, you might want to put pressure on the in [index] finger, off-center the ball, or try no seams," Cairncross said. "A different arm angle, again, that might help. Turning the ball over might help you too."

Although pitchers aren't supposed to be merely a "one-pitch" pitcher, some men get away with it more or less. In 2002, Pirates closer Mike Williams was among the best in the game with 46 saves, trailing only John Smoltz and Eric Gagne for NL leadership. And he did it mainly with the slider.

"It's no secret that I throw a slider, that's my pitch," he said of his pitch that looks like a fastball when it leaves his hand, but takes a nasty, down-and-away break just as it arrives at the plate. Williams continued, "The hitters know it, my teammates know it, everybody knows it." No reliever ever had more saves on a losing team than Williams, and only one ever saved a higher percentage of his team's victories than this underappreciated bullpen inhabitant (63.9 percent).

An Associated Press article compared Williams's reliance upon his slider to Trevor Hoffman's dependence upon his changeup, since both men lack a 95 mph blazer. Williams has pondered his fate, saying, "Why can't I throw Greg Maddux's sinker? But everybody's different, and I believe that's why my slider is mine. I don't think anybody can throw it the way I can. It's not a trick pitch, it's just the way I throw it and hold it."

It's been estimated he throws his best pitch about 75 percent of the time. That, he said, makes it challenging to adapt to the hitters' adjustments. He must grope to find new ways of getting the batters out, such as mixing up his rare off pitches. He began to show more fastballs to righties and more changes to lefties so they couldn't anticipate the slider as readily.

However, in 2003, he seemed to forget his fastball entirely; by July he had an inflated ERA of 6.29 yet had 24 saves. At the time *USA Today Sports Weekly* reported that no pitcher had ever gone an entire season with 20+ saves with an ERA over 6.00.

Pittsburgh manager Lloyd McClendon commented, "It's understandable why Mike would rely on his slider because it is such a great pitch. I really believe, though, that a pitcher needs to work off his fastball in the National League to be successful."

Likewise, Atlanta's Smoltz mainly goes fastball-slider. He still gets away with it, said Smith, because "both of his pitches are above average. As a closer, you can get away with it if you have one [pitch] if you have a very good fastball with life on it.

"Bryan Harvey had a forkball as good as a fastball, same speed and he kept it in the zone. And that was the key to him, keeping the ball down and making his fastball look like a forkball and vice versa. If you have an above-average fastball, you can get away with that with a decent backup pitch."

One nearly unique style of pitching belonged to Kansas City's Dan Quisenberry, who used a wide array of pitches while throwing submarine-style to baffle hitters. With great control, he'd mix up his pitches effectively. One time he struck out Rickey Henderson on a knuckleball. Henderson mused, "I didn't know he had a knuckleball until he threw me one with two strikes. I had no chance. I just froze and let it go by. I stared at him, but he just turned his back. I went back to the dugout thinking, 'That's not fair.'"

In 2003, Danny Graves was making the transition from closer to starter for his Reds. So accustomed was he to working out of the stretch, he struggled in the spring when going from the windup. By late March he said he was considering pitching from the stretch at all times. Many relievers refuse to work from the windup even with no men on base, but starters seldom do this. When Yankee Don Larsen threw his perfect game in the World Series, though, he used a rare no-windup style.

Staying sharp and/or getting help from others pays off. For example, if a batter changes his stance or where he stands in the box, making a slight adjustment to the pitcher, does the pitcher usually spot this and attempt to counteract the move? San Diego pitcher Brian Lawrence said, "Maybe not so much a stance. It would depend more on his swing than where he was set up in the box. If he was getting better swings on a particular pitch, then we would adjust that way more [than with] a particular stance — maybe the stance leads to the swing, but it's the whole package, and not just where he's setting up."

If a hitter moved up in the box, Lawrence said his catcher would pick up on that "better than I would, being right there next to him, he'd get an idea that if he's moving up, maybe he thinks something is coming and the catcher might not call that pitch."

As far as the batter moving in on the plate or moving a bit away from the plate, Lawrence said he'd notice that immediately, but his reaction would depend on certain factors. "If I'm throwing away, away, away, and he's scooting up [on the plate] in the box, then definitely you can't throw the same pitch because [then] it's going to be more or less down the middle to him. You definitely adjust to the guy moving up on the plate more than you would moving back off the plate, because then I would just throw a ball inside instead of throwing it over the plate and just hope he swings at it."

Reed said if hitters crowd the plate on him, he will come in tight. "I think each pitcher's got his own different makeup. I'm going to try to control the inside part of the plate and whatever that takes to do, [I'll do it]. Nowadays you don't see that, you see guys [hitters] falling out over the middle of the plate and doing what they want, but I think it has to do with a lot of [pitchers'] personalities—each individual. Some guys are afraid of throwing in; other guys are kind of old school, they take that part of the plate."

Pitching tight is something tons of young pitchers often neglect nowadays. The common theory for this phenomenon is that they didn't throw inside during their years prior to making it to the professional level because the batters they had faced had all been armed with aluminum bats. Due to the advent of that weapon, today's multitude of strong hitters, even when jammed, still make enough contact so that the bat does much of the work and the ball sails into the outfield for a hit.

It's the inverse of Pavlov's salivating dogs: pitchers who throw to a specific zone, only to find failure, will "extinguish" such behavior and, in this case, abandon the concept of throwing inside to batters.

Another reason suggested as to why some pitchers don't throw tight nowadays is because they lack the control to brush batters off the plate without hitting them and giving them a free trip to first base. Still, those who have the control and the heart to throw in do get the stimulus-response reward of winning games at the big-league level. Perhaps the best four masters of inside pitching today are Roger Clemens, Randy Johnson, Curt Schilling, and Pedro Martinez.

So for those who feel pitchers nowadays are timid, these pitchers have a rebuttal. A Martinez rebuttal travels at over 90 mph and is sometimes aimed at the batter's head—truly a very convincing argument.

Slugger Mo Vaughn told *USA Today Baseball Weekly* that Martinez is the kind of pitcher who will "back you out of the box if he has to. You won't get the whole plate against him."

As for Clemens, Tino Martinez told *Sports Illustrated* that the "Rocket" is unafraid to throw tight, but he also has "enough control to come right back with a pitch on the outside corner. That's how he controls the game."

By the same token, Lawrence asserted, "I definitely will come inside. I think my stats reflect that—I've hit a lot of guys and, you know, it's not intentional. It's just a matter of you've got to get it in there, because if you leave it out over the plate, they'll hit it out of the park. If I'm going to miss, I'm going to miss on their side so they're going to get nicked here and there; that's just the way it is. I'm not scared to do it." In April 2003, he tied the major league record for the most men hit by a pitch in an inning with three.

"And, you know," he continued, "sometimes now the game dictates [it] because the umpires are throwing warnings out there and if you hit the next guy, then you're out of the ball game. You try not to take that chance but sometimes you just gotta do it and whatever happens, happens."

Reliever Scott Stewart agrees with Lawrence. "I think we still pitch in." He said a pitcher simply has to do this—otherwise the hitters would control nearly all of home plate and pitchers simply can't let that happen.

While Lawrence has never hit the plate-hugging, "Armor All"–wearing Barry Bonds with a pitch, he said of Bonds: "he's so far up on the plate, I try to get it [the ball] in there, but sometimes you don't. You definitely tense up a little more when a guy like him comes in the batter's box. You try to go a little bit extra 'out of the bag,' but sometimes that hurts you more than helps you."

Plus, pitchers don't tend to hit Bonds all that often. Brent Butler, now with the Cardinals, theorized that Bonds has earned respect from pitchers around the league, but added that, yes, there is an element of fear for pitchers. "He's a big guy," he said with a laugh.

It seems odd, though, that pitchers such as the aggressive Early Wynn and Don Drysdale felt that they owned the plate (or at least most of it), but gradually, in a sort of devolution, most pitchers have seemingly allowed, or were forced to give, batters the inside part of the plate.

Furthermore, according to at least one hitter, if, somehow, pitchers took back the plate and began to dust hitters off, they'd come to accept it. Butler conceded he would probably adapt to that change, "because you look back in the old days and you hear stories all the time about how they threw inside—brushback, knockdown, and it was part of the game. But I guess it's just the way the game has changed and the way it's being played these days compared to back then. Maybe it's just a different style."

Lawrence added, "When you're trying to hit a guy, everybody knows it—something happened [like the other team plunked your star player], but that's something [payback] that you have to do. But if you're just pitching inside and you nick a couple of guys . . ." his voice trailed off before he concluded, "Ah, people read into it too much."

Beanballs and knockdowns aside, to be effective, a pitcher should, at least on occasion, keep a hitter honest by throwing the ball in on him. While it seems obvious that, by and large, pitchers are afraid now to throw in, when interviewed most pitchers claim otherwise. In some cases, there is no doubt about it. Again, Martinez has, from his early years on, come in on (and often nipped or drilled) hitters. He took a lot of heat for this and was labeled a brash upstart, but he continued to use both the inside and outside corners. Further, he continued to win big.

Styles change over the years. Most pitchers today, accustomed to a five-man staff, prefer not to work without at least four days of rest. There are, of course, exceptions. Down the tense stretch drive of the 2000 season, Cleveland's Chuck Finley stepped it up a notch and not only glistened (6–1 overall in September), but also won his last two starts, in enormously vital games with three days' rest. He explained, "It's all mental. I guess the fourth day just gives you more time to worry."

His manager back then, Manuel, said some pitchers such as Finley "bounce back good" and are able to work on short rest. He also said, "Fifteen, twenty years ago, there were four-man rotations, and everybody pitched on three days' rest." Obviously, times change and so do pitching philosophies and strategies.

There are exceptions, though. Through the 2002 season, Maddux had a career ledger of 19–6 over 34 starts when working on three days' rest. That was good for a .760 won-loss percentage as compared to his .635 in all other starts.

Then, of course, there were the pitchers from long ago. Way back in 1934, the rubber-armed Paige said, "I sure get laughs when I see in the papers where some major league pitcher says he gets a sore arm because he's overworked, and he pitches every four days. Man, that'd be a vacation for me." That's no exaggeration, considering that Paige once pitched in 165 games in a row during his barnstorming days.

Paige clearly felt that pitchers were becoming pampered. "Pitchers today," he summed up in 1981, "have arm trouble because they sit on the bench and don't work enough." In his youth, Cy Young frequently pitched on two days' rest en route to chalking up the all-time win total of 511, now considered one of sport's unbreakable records.

A huge part of today's pitching game is keeping track of pitch counts for starters and limiting their time on the hill by the number of pitches thrown. Old-timers such as Bob Feller, Gaylord Perry, and Sandy Koufax have disdain for the coddling of pitchers, because they preferred to go the distance in their own starts.

In a *Baseball Digest* article, Jerome Holtzman quoted Koufax as saying, "To me, a quality start is when the starting pitcher is still on the mound when the game is over and his teammates rush out of the dugout to congratulate him on a victory." None of this six innings of giving up three runs or less for him.

However, today's pitchers are brought along differently than the Koufaxes were. The new breed of pitchers are protected and seldom throw 110–140 pitches in a game. In Leo Mazzone's book *Pitch Like a Pro*, he conceded that the Braves also pay attention to the number of pitches their starters throw, limiting them to around 125 pitches. While some men such as Johnson are occasionally given the go-ahead to work up in the 130–140s, Mazzone feels it is usually bad news to let a pitcher work over 140.

Not only do managers pamper their pitchers as far as the pitch count goes, they also bring their young pitchers along slowly, limiting also their yearly innings pitched. When Joel Pineiro was in his first full season, his manager, Piniella, said he didn't want "to wear him down." He wanted to keep Pineiro's workload to around 175 innings.

With this type of thinking prevailing now, the 300-innings pitcher for a season is also a thing of the past. Holtzman said that before pitches were officially logged, some writers recalled Ryan once throwing as many as 259 pitches in a 12-inning contest, and toiling through 332 total innings in 1974. Hardly babied, Ryan lasted in the majors until he was a Methuselah-like 44 years of age.

Since pitchers don't work as deep into games as they once did, complete games today are about as scarce as unicorns. Feller told about how things have changed. "It used to be expected that a starting pitcher would pace himself and make it through the complete game if he possibly could. Nowadays the manager tells him, 'Go out and give it everything on every pitch! That's why we have a bullpen.' So, after say six innings, the pitcher's looking over his shoulder for some relief, whether he needs it or not. In addition, my personal view is that the pitchers don't have as much stamina as they used to have."

Amazingly, the pre-1900 record for complete games in a season is 74 and the "modern" high is 48, set by Jack Chesbro in 1904. By way of comparison, Randy Johnson led the major leagues in 2003 with a mere 8 complete games.

Hal Bock of the Associated Press wrote of Warren Spahn leading the National League in complete games in 1963 with 22—at the unbelievable age of 42. Bock quoted Yankees manager Joe Torre as saying, "It's a different game than it was 20 years ago. It's a game of specialization now. You have your starter, your set-up man, your closer, and you structure the game that way." Torre said he lets a starter get a complete game only if his pitch count is very low.

Bock also wrote, "Thirty years ago, when the designated hitter was introduced, 27.3 percent of starts were complete games. That dropped to 17.7 in 1983, 8.2 in 1993, and has been below 5 percent every year since 1999."

Final case in point. In August of 2002, Mark Prior K'd 12 batters, a very nifty career high for a rookie. He left after six innings and just 105 spent pitches because manager Bruce Kimm said he wanted to monitor his protégé. In fact, General Manager Jim Hendry said of the 21-year-old star, "There's no way Mark Prior was going to be overloaded and get in 200-plus innings as a rookie." He said that they would shut his season down before hitting the 200 plateau. In college Prior had never worked more than 138⅔ innings.

It's hard to believe Pineiro and Prior were playing the same sport as old-timer Charles "Old Hoss" Radbourne, a pitcher who went 60–12 while starting and completing 73 of his team's 112 games back in 1884, totaling an astonishing 678⅔ innings that year (all for a salary of $3,000).

2

Pitching Theories

SATCHEL PAIGE NEVER took the ACT or the SAT, but he had a Ph.D. in pitching. He rattled off bits of advice with the insight of a philosopher. He not only gave us the classic "don't look back" line, he also concocted many concise insights dealing with the art of pitching. He felt it was important to conserve energy, saying pitchers should avoid running and rigorous exercise at all times. He even joked, "I believe in training by rising gently up and down from the bench."

Bob Gibson spoke more seriously about his philosophy of pitching: "On an 0-2 count, throw your best fastball or slider. Don't lay it in there when you've got 0-2 on the batter. Ninety percent of the time if you throw fastballs pretty good, down the middle, but with stuff on it, they'll foul it off. But pitchers are getting too cute and go deeper in the count now." Gibson clearly did not believe in wasting pitches; he'd challenge a batter.

Warren Spahn held to a theory that resulted in him throwing high pitches quite often to hitters who bent their back knee; he saw them as low-ball hitters. Conversely, he said, "If he's hitting off his front foot, he's a high-ball hitter."

He was also wise enough to know that if a pitcher misses his location, he's better off missing outside the batter's hot zone, and better off missing low than high.

Meanwhile, standout starter Mike Mussina says he figures out how he wants to pitch the enemy based on experience, and "then I try to read what a guy's doing while he's standing up there at the plate. Every situation is different."

He emphasized that on a given day he might not have his good breaking ball or change, and, since he doesn't throw 97 mph, he studies what happens in the first inning. He focuses on "what I see the batters doing—are they swinging early in the count or are they trying to work the count?"

Often, paradoxically, two theories that both make sense, clash. Some pitchers feel they should concentrate on their strengths early in the count. If they work a batter into a hole, they may then consider working to that hitter's weakness.

Other pitchers say they almost always throw or emphasize their best stuff, not worrying at all about the hitters' weaknesses. That is especially true if that weakness is for a pitch that isn't the pitcher's forte.

In August of 2000 Paul Shuey, then in the Cleveland bullpen, spoke about his approach to pitching. He was asked if he, armed with such a nasty splitter, felt that he would mainly stick with that effective pitch when he was in a crucial situation. He replied, "I'm real close to that [thinking] especially toward playoffs. I'll really pay more attention to where a guy doesn't hit the ball real well consistently, and I might try to refine my pitches a little bit [against him] to get him in a certain spot. But for the most part, I'm going to stay with my strengths most of the year."

Many experts believe that decisions such as Shuey spoke of should belong to the pitcher. Clyde King told writer Bob Cairns that when he was a young pitcher, he once threw 12 straight fastballs to Mel Ott before the slugger connected for a bases-loaded double. When team executive Branch Rickey called in King to ask him why he didn't mix in a curve or two, King informed Rickey that he was simply following the orders of his catcher. Rickey quickly set King straight, saying, "You're the boss on the mound. The catcher does not dictate! He suggests. If you agree, fine. If you don't, just shake your head."

Then there's another element that Mazzone stresses to his pitchers: mixing up speeds. Of course this idea is nothing new. Well over fifty years ago Spahn, another famous Brave, commented, "Hitting is timing. Pitching is upsetting timing."

"Sudden" Sam McDowell, who possessed an ungodly fastball and twice blew the ball by more than 300 batters in a season, was asked how he'd work Tony Gwynn. The lefty, who led his league in strikeouts five times, said, "In my particular case, with my fastball, and knowing he has a weakness up and in, I'd throw him hard fastballs up and in. Oh, I'd keep him honest, too, with changeups away."

Carl Erskine, a Dodger great from the 1950s era, said during a late 1990s interview that when it comes to pitching technique, he believes in another truism. "There's a basic standard in pitching—pitch high and tight, and low and away. You can also change speeds. I think it still applies."

Still, if a pitcher could truly master control so well that, on any pitch, he could put the ball in or out, up or down, and then add variations to the speed and break of the ball, he would be a robot and not a human. Some pitchers like Maddux come close to this level of perfection, but all pitchers make mistakes, of course.

Another ancient theory is never to let the other team's star beat you. In 2002, Barry Bonds set World Series records for the most walks drawn (13), most intentional walks (7), and the most intentional walks issued in a single Series game (3). Incredibly, during his first nine plate appearance in the World Series, he saw exactly 10 strikes.

Further, in 17 postseason games he was given 17 free passes. For that matter, after he hit his record 73 home runs in 2001, virtually every pitcher respected and avoided Bonds as he drew a single season record 198 walks. Pitchers felt vindicated in walking him because he scored on just 34 occasions after taking a free pass.

Coming off a season in which he drew all those walks, with 68 being of the intentional variety, good for another record, Bonds read in newspapers that the Anaheim Angels starting pitcher in Game 1 of the Series also planned on being cautious. Jarrod Washburn said, "If the situation calls for pitching around him, I have to swallow my pride a little bit and be smart. If the situation calls for me to walk him, I'll check my ego at the door." He also said, "Hopefully, he'll come up every time with nobody on base and we get to go after him. That's ultimately what I would like to happen."

In their first confrontation, Washburn should have also checked his definition of what a "situation" is—he threw a pitch Bonds could pull and the Giants slugger cracked a solo home run. At that rate, had Washburn continued to get his wish to face Bonds with no one on, Bonds would have homered repeatedly. In a game that wound up being a one-run contest, the homer definitely hurt, though Washburn and the Angels eventually won the series.

Now, even though Cook has said he, too, respects Bonds, just before the 2002 Series started, he said he would pitch to him, but added that he knew he'd have "to be smart with him."

Angels manager Mike Scioscia was more moderate, saying his strategy would depend upon the situation, including how the hitter after Bonds was faring. Even Cook conceded, "Late in the game with a base open, you don't pitch to Barry. One out and a runner on early in the game, you pitch to him." Pitching coach Bud Black added, "If there's two outs in a scoreless game, I assume we'd pitch to him. Two-out walks haunt."

The final word came from Scott Schoeneweis. "The best-case scenario," he began, "is to get the guys out before Barry comes up."

On August 16, 2002, a relatively unknown pitcher for the Florida Marlins, Michael Tejera, faced and defeated Bonds and his Giants, 4–2. One reason Tejera topped them was he pitched smart, avoiding throwing strikes to the torrid Bonds. As a matter of fact, of the 13 pitches he offered to Bonds, 12 were out of the strike zone. He refused to give in to Bonds, giving him nothing he could handle during his first three trips to the plate (with at least one runner on base each time). Had he thrown Bonds a pitch to his liking, and had he homered on such a pitch, Tejera could not have achieved his two-run-margin win.

By the way, despite his clever tactics and his earning the victory, the fans in Miami booed their own pitcher as their bloodlust, their desire to see a Bonds home run, overcame them.

Lawrence said that he has no qualms about pitching around a man such as Bonds (not that there are that many hitters like Bonds). "If it's a close game and I think this guy's going to knock it out of the park or get a hit to score some runs, and there's an open base, I'm not going to take the chance. Why not take the next guy?

"In that respect, you definitely [must be cautious]. I did it the other night, I pitched around [Robbie] Alomar with a guy on third and I ended up getting a double play to end the inning with no runs scored. You definitely do it and it doesn't matter really who the hitter is if you think he's going to do the job and you can get the next guy out, you pitch around him a little bit."

That tied in with one of Paige's many theories, one that qualifies as an aphorism: "If a man can beat you, walk him."

Sounds logical, but St. Louis Cardinals great Red Schoendienst said that back in his playing days pitchers couldn't avoid pitching to such stars, simply because "there were a lot, especially when there were only eight teams. You'd go into Brooklyn and you'd have [Roy] Campanella, [Duke] Snider, and [Gil] Hodges. Every team had some guys that you knew you couldn't get away with saying, 'The pitcher's gonna pitch around this guy,' because you'd have to pitch around the next one and the next one [too]."

In the meantime, Ted Williams once revealed a pitching theory that could, to some extent, thwart even the great "Splendid Splinter." He believed it helped pitchers to throw different ways, with different deliveries, motions, or tempos—à la Paige or Luis Tiant. Anything that disrupted the hitter's concentration was a bonus for the pitcher, contended Williams.

One theory that Glavine has pertains to umps. He confessed that he will test the home plate umpire by trying to "see how much I can get away with." Like teammate Maddux, Glavine conceded that, in part due to his star status, he gets strikes called for him that are actually outside the strike zone. He just isn't sure until the umpire makes calls on a given night how much leeway he will have. It's the old "give him an inch, he'll take a mile" scenario, and Glavine is adept at testing the boundaries, be it an inch or a figurative mile.

In the old days of the game a catcher would pretty much sit squarely behind the plate. He would indicate if he wanted the pitcher to go inside or outside, or high versus low by simply motioning with a finger or by moving his mitt but not his body (at least not much). Now, says catcher Michael Barrett, "the game has come down to a matter of inches and the focus on certain hitters is in or out, not so much up or down. About twenty years ago the focus was more on keeping the ball down, down, down; now you're starting to see guys get away from that."

He said current thinking of pitching strategy includes the idea of "pitch a guy inside or pitch a guy outside, it doesn't really matter—if you make the pitch, you can get the guy out." So working in and out seems to matter more if, again, the pitcher executes the pitch, than keeping the ball low. The key, of course, is making the pitch, not a mistake that a batter will devour.

In his book *Pure Baseball*, All-Star Keith Hernandez said that another theory of pitching is if a batter likes to take a pitch and go away with it to the opposite field, then "you might as well pitch him out there, play him that way in the outfield. It's the pitch a batter away and play him away concept," Hernandez said. In theory, it works. Of course, pitchers are human and may miss on their location, but the logic of this concept remains solid.

A classic example, though, of how any theory can break down is the Gwynn case. Everyone knew he liked to take the outside pitch and dump it into left field, but, for some reason, teams didn't effectively guard against this when facing Gwynn. In fact, he said that Bonds was the only left fielder who played the great Padre hitter in, daring him to drive the ball over his head.

Still, perhaps the simple truth is that against some hitters no theory works completely. With a guy like Gwynn, a pitcher was in a Lincolnesque situation: You can defend some of the hitters some of the time, and you can defend some of the hitters all the time, but you can't defend Gwynn. Still, one doesn't throw out a legitimate theory merely because of one superlative hitter.

McDowell was a four-time strikeout leader during the 1960s. In 1965, he led the AL in ERA, and his 325 strikeouts still ranks as the most ever by a Cleveland lefty. His fastball was his best pitch, but he insisted on going after batters with his curveball, too. "It's no fun throwing fastballs to guys who can't hit them," he supposedly said. "The real challenge is getting them out on stuff they can hit." He also is said to have joked once about the mind games that go on between hitters and pitchers. "Trying to think with me is a mismatch. Most of the time I don't know where the pitch is going."

Incidentally, he also once refuted his quote about his propensity for going after hitters with his second-best pitch. "People always stereotype players, make generalizations," he said somewhat defensively. "Very few people realize for my entire career every pitch was called for by my manager." He admitted that the bum rap used to upset him, "but there was nothing I could do about it, so why let it bother me?"

In the meantime, Charles Nagy, who was a mainstay of the Cleveland Indians' rotation in the 1990s, said that there are some basic lessons all young pitchers breaking into the majors should learn. "You have to have command of certain pitches. You have to have the command of your fastball, being able to throw it to both sides of the plate. And you have to be able to throw a breaking ball for a strike, be able to use it, and throw it for an out pitch. If you can't do those things, right away you're going to have a really tough time."

Eddie Perez has had the good luck and skill to catch some of baseball's greatest pitchers. As a member of the perennial winners, the Atlanta Braves, he was on the receiving end of Maddux, Smoltz, and Glavine.

He said the Braves staff has been so successful "because they throw strikes. They throw strikes all the time, and on both sides of the plate. They never throw the ball in the middle.

"The first thing [discussed] when we were doing a meeting was, 'Throw strike one to get this thing going. Get ahead of the hitters and then do whatever they want.'"

Plus, he said, it wasn't just the stars who would do this; it was everybody. The secondary stars on the staff would see the great stuff and strategy of the Cy Young–caliber pitchers and "would follow them because they were successful at doing that. That's why you see veteran guys go out there and have great years [even as newcomers]."

He gave the example of the year John Burkett had after coming off several substandard seasons. When he came to the Braves, he enjoyed some success "because he tried to do it like them. He was throwing strike one and then pitched from there. That's the big tip on pitching, I think."

Young pitchers need to learn new philosophies as well. They must realize quickly that in order to go up the ladder of the minors and make it to the Show, according to coach and former infielder Robby Thompson, they have to know that "there's no doubt [big-league pitchers'] command of their pitches [is better], that's why they're up here. That's how you get up here, basically [by] hitting spots and [having] command.

"You watch games and when pitchers do that, they win or at least they're in the ball game. When pitchers do not hit spots, they get whacked around a little bit."

Part of evolving into a quality pitcher is coping with pressure and nerves. Actually, even after becoming a name pitcher, butterflies can play havoc with a player's gut. Even though Kenny Rogers had developed enough to become a recognizable name, he admits that during his perfect game he was nervous. "I tried not to dwell on it and just tried to stay focused on just getting people out and making pitches, and that was a big benefit that my focus never wavered to a negative thought the whole game—without a doubt, not one time.

"I don't think it was just one pitch or anything else like that [as a key], but it was more mental than anything. I think my focus was so good that it didn't matter what pitch I threw, I believed in it and I knew I was going to throw it good."

Rogers also cited a fundamental of pitching that he felt came to him rather late in his career, but could help a young pitcher enormously. He cautioned that all too often young pitchers won't listen to advice that is so different from what they, in their youthful exuberance, feel has to be right. "For me, the best thing that I've learned, basically recently, is as a pitcher, be a pitcher. And I go out there sometimes and try to throw the ball and overpower a hitter, and I don't have that kind of stuff, and not many people do, but you [should] stay in control and not get out of your comfort level or comfort zone of how you pitch. You're going to make more mistakes when you get out of your comfortable zone." As a rule, it takes time for a young pitcher to be smart, to trust himself, and, again, to pitch, not merely heave the ball.

Rogers, employing the wisdom of age, uses guile and loves to face hitters who try to "swing too hard, try and pull the ball too much." Those are the ones he says who "get themselves out most of the time."

Palmer, who never dished up a grand slam over his long, illustrious 19-year career, took a definite approach to the game. For one thing, he did not like to issue intentional walks. He explained why in his book *Pitching*.

First, he wanted to avoid big innings, and freely putting men on increased the chances of such an occurrence. Second, he wrote, "When you intentionally walk somebody, you create a situation where you have to pitch to the next batter—you can't pitch carefully and you can't pitch around him."

Palmer also felt that when it came to strategy on the mound, a pitcher should never throw a waste pitch—every pitch must have a reason behind it. He wrote, "If I decide to throw the pitch [on an 0-2 count] low and away, it's not my intention merely to throw it for a ball. I want to make it very close to the strike zone, with the idea of getting the batter to look for the ball away." Then he would come up and in on the next pitch to fool the batter he had just set up. He tried never to throw a ball, say, eight inches off the plate, a pitch so far out of the zone that the hitter isn't tempted to bite—that, Palmer felt, was truly a wasted pitch, serving no purpose at all.

Now, when he was behind in the count, say at 2-0, he knew hitters were sitting on a fastball, so he often came in with his slider. Hitters often would swing at the slider, as it looks like a fastball at first, only to hit it off the end of the bat for a harmless out.

A 300-game winner, Early Wynn employed a theory that defied most pitching conventions. He frequently ran the count on hitters deep, often to a full count. He would get ahead early in the count, then nibble, refusing to give batters good pitches to hit. Walks, then, were inevitable; when he retired he had walked more men than any pitcher ever (a record since broken by Nolan Ryan).

Meanwhile, a Wynn teammate, Bob Feller, said that if he had a comfortable lead in a contest, he'd take something off his pitches, not wanting to strain his valuable arm. "A lot of guys can win, but can't win 1–0 games. I'd pace myself. If I had a lead, I'd ease up. Then you can bear down on tough guys or save yourself for the next game. I didn't care about ERA, but it takes time to learn this."

He said he honestly didn't care if he'd give up a few unnecessary runs, even if it meant inflating his earned run average, as long as he could stay out there on the mound and help his Indians win. As he put it, "The bottom line is, did you win or lose? What's more important, having a low ERA or a high one and win?" Actually, Feller, who sounded like he could pitch on cruise control, managed to achieve the best of both worlds. He won, to the tune of 266 games, and had a minuscule ERA (3.25 for his 18-year career).

Roger Craig's book *Inside Pitch* supports Feller's perspective. "Most pitchers deliberately alter their pattern of pitching when a game is not on the line. Why show a hitter your best stuff when the game is out of reach?"

Many pitchers try to set hitters up. Palmer went so far as to show a batter a pitch in spring training in certain situations just to get him to think later, in the regular season, that he might see that same pitch. He probably never would.

Ryan, known more for speed than off-speed stuff, believed that a changeup should be about 15 mph slower than a pitcher's fastball. In *Nolan Ryan's Pitcher's Bible*, he stated, "Ten mph below the fastball is OK, but only if the pitch is low and in the strike zone."

Also, since pitchers often are vulnerable in the first inning, Ryan noted, "My goal is to escape the first inning without giving up any runs, establish the tone of the game, gain the confidence of my teammates, and build my own confidence."

Further, since he knew that a high percentage of leadoff batters who get on base in any inning wind up scoring, Ryan also worked hard at preventing those hitters from reaching base.

The Jack Armstrong credo was one of hard work. The right-handed pitcher said, "I'm proud of just giving everything I've got every day, of my persistence and attention to dedication day in and day out. I just want to get in the 35 or so starts they give me and give them quality starts, to try to keep the team in the game. No quitting."

Then there was Alan Mills, who had been both a starter and a reliever. He revealed that when he was a starter his approach in the late innings was the same as it was in the early innings. "I didn't try to do anything different," he said, but admitted many other pitchers feel another way. Most pitchers believe they must change as the game goes on. In fact, pitching coach Dick Pole said a pitcher just about has to change something starting with the second time through the batting order.

In *The Superstar Hitter's Bible*, Bernardo Leonard wrote that pitchers frequently don't want to throw a strike. In theory pitchers should always "throw the ball near the plate, around the plate, at the edge of the plate in an attempt to get you to swing at a pitch you won't be comfortable swinging at. The pitches that most often get you [a hitter] out are the ones that look hittable but aren't."

All-time Yankee great Whitey Ford offered a different approach. "You would be amazed," he said, "how many important outs you can get by working the count down to where the hitter is sure you're going to throw to his weakness, and then throw to his power instead."

Clyde Wright said that he often thought three pitches ahead of the batter. He also tried to record outs on around five pitches or less. He noted that the flamethrowers wind up with more foul balls being ticked and ultimately that builds up the pitch count and strain on the pitcher's arm.

His theory was that when a pitcher mastered his art, it became fun on the mound, fooling hitters, rather than trying to blow it by them. "If he's looking for a fastball," Wright started, "you throw him a changeup. You just go the opposite way. Then one time he's sitting there thinking, 'He's not going to throw me a fastball,' then you throw a little fastball on him. It's fun to try to outfox a hitter."

Maddux also had an interesting theory on what it takes to register a fine record over the course of a season. To him, the key difference between, for instance, a .500 record and a sparkling one was, "You have to win 2–1 or 3–2." To do so five or six times per season will result in a fine won-loss slate. While that's easier said than performed, his concept is well taken.

He elaborated, "People can say what they want about run support. You're going to have your games where you get seven or eight runs, but it's the games where you get two or three that make a difference in the year you're going to have."

Lee Smith added yet another thought: the pitcher shouldn't be the man on the field to feel fear—it should be the batter that's on the defensive. When someone told Smith to beware of a player because he was a good fastball hitter, he retorted, "OK, let him hit the ball. You got defense there; you got nine on one—the percentages don't get any better than that. I figure I can win nine on one. Things are looking pretty good if I make quality pitches. They're going to get you sometimes, but with good pitches, you're going to win."

Another key that great pitchers all realize is, as Smith stated, "Stay away from that crooked number. If you have an inning where you're going to give up a run, if you stay away from the crooked number [higher than a single run], you're looking pretty good. If I go out there [in relief] with the bases loaded, no outs, and I give up one run, I'm real happy. But you go out there and drop a two here and a three here and a four there, you're not going to win the game.

"A good starting pitcher will give up a [single] run every now and then, but he's going to win because most teams now in the big leagues have a pretty good offense."

3

Preparation and Training

MANY PEOPLE HAVE the conception that players today don't discuss or critique their games with teammates as a method of improving their craft. Sam McDowell says that's nonsense. "Old-timers say over and over that players nowadays don't talk baseball. What they really mean is [talking baseball] in a bar. Modern players don't want to sit around a bar—they're more sophisticated about health. They talk over breakfast, lunch, or dinner.

"In the past, players *would* talk about the game. You'd have six, seven guys who'd love to sit around two, three hours after the game. They'd be talking, but while drinking free beers in the locker."

Curt Schilling developed into a great pitcher for many reasons. One was the fact that he was willing to take lessons from the masters of the game—most notably Roger Clemens. As a matter of fact, their confab a handful of years ago has become part of the Schilling lore. It was said that he listened intently and soaked up advice with the absorption of a Bounty paper towel.

Maddux is another opponent who has shared his expertise with Schilling. "I'm not even on the same team, and I learn from the guy. I pick his brain as often as I can.

"I mean, you're talking about a guy who has been the best pitcher in the game for the last 15 years. He has dominated the game the last 15 years like nobody else."

Nagy grew up in the same apartment building as Tom Seaver and used to bother him with autograph requests. Years later he ran into Seaver. "He came over doing the radio for a game and I talked to him beforehand," Nagy said. "Mostly he made small talk, but it never hurts to seek out a great and hear his words of insight."

Smith has a unique way to prepare as a pitcher. He recalled, "Billy Williams used to give me a hard time about why I would be [sitting in on] hitters' meetings. I said, 'I want to know what you guys are thinking when the game's on the line.' You don't find pitchers that will go to hitters' meetings—I was the only pitcher sitting in there. It wasn't because I thought I was going to be facing my teammates [someday], it was because I wanted to know what Ryne Sandberg and Ron Cey, Davey Lopes, all those guys were looking for in a key situation. So I learned a lot about pitching by talking to hitters."

Many fans felt Smith was all power and no prep, but that simply wasn't true. "I tell you what, when I went between the lines, I was prepared. I didn't have to tell everybody what I did. When the end of the season came, and I was in the top three or four in saves, [it all paid off]."

When he'd face a hitter for the first time and wasn't armed with much data about that man's tendencies, strengths, and weaknesses, he was still ready. He said, "That was my whole reason for watching batting practice. I'd also talk to some of our young guys at the pitchers' meeting and we'd go over the new guys before that first time around. 'Does anybody know this guy?'

"I remember one guy that I didn't know and I came out [onto the field] and he's hitting about eight balls into the center field bleachers for the White Sox. It was Dan Pasqua. And I'm like, 'Who is this guy?'" He was informed that Pasqua was on the disabled list. "He could hit [those shots] at Fenway and he's not even on the team?

"Those guys like that, that I didn't know, I would watch them take batting practice and I'd find out their number and look over their roster." If the new man was just coming up to the majors, Smith would ask young teammates who might have known that hitter from their days in the minors. If the hitter Smith wasn't familiar with was a veteran, perhaps one Smith hadn't been in the same league with before, he'd then ask a veteran teammate for advice.

While Smith learned a lot from seeing hitters' tendencies, styles, and swings in BP, he admitted he could be fooled. "I'll tell you what, Eddie Murray was the worst batting practice hitting fellow I've ever seen in my life. He got jammed all the time, but when 7:05 [game time] came around, he was a pretty bad man; he was ready. I don't know if he was jammed intentionally or if he was just trying to work on muscling the ball, but he took some ugly batting practice."

After seeing a hitter get jammed in practice, a pitcher might predict he'd be an easy out. When Smith saw how good Murray actually was, he smiled then muttered incredulously, "This guy's the best hitter I've seen in years and he's like a pitcher up there hitting. He just didn't hit the ball with authority like I knew he did during the game."

Rogers observed, "Pitchers can learn from hitters just like hitters can learn from pitchers. You try and pick their brain just to find out what they might do in certain situations." Often a pitcher will ask hitters about "what they're looking for."

Such information is instantly stored away in the pitcher's data bank. "Any kind of insight you get as a pitcher into a hitter's mind can only benefit you." Further, Rogers insists one is never too old to learn. In 2002, at the age of 37, he said, "I still do it. I ask as many questions as anybody, probably. More than probably any young guys, but I still feel there's always a way to improve or make an adjustment to where you can go out there and be successful."

He said that most of his team's young players seek him out. He noted, "Usually they just watch, just seeing what you do [and] how you do it, but I think they probably get more from watching than talking to you—your mannerisms out there and when you do get in certain situations, how you cope with it. Some guys get a little anxious and you can tell; you can tell when people get a little nervous out there and it doesn't help you — it hurts you." Again, that's a lesson that's easy to tell a young player, but it's also one that takes years to assimilate. Rogers said he wishes he could impart his knowledge to young pitchers, but sometimes a player has to learn things on his own.

Some players not only talk to others, they even talk to themselves, whispering little reminders such as, "Relax, stay within yourself." None was more famous for this than Detroit's Mark "The Bird" Fidrych. A few players have even employed forms of hypnosis, notably the eccentric Bill Faul — but lacking a good fastball, all the prep in the world couldn't help this 12–16 lifetime pitcher.

In *Pen Men* by Bob Cairns, catcher Tim McCarver spoke of how Hall of Famer Steve Carlton used psychological techniques. He prepared in the bullpen prior to a start where, before picking up the ball, he would "go into a trance like state." McCarver said he was picturing the outside and inside portions of home plate "under the theory that thought precedes action and you keep the ball away from the fat part of the plate."

McDowell said that when he played he tried to help himself become a better player by reading books on sports psychology. Not only did that make him different from his peers, he became a sort of pariah in the eyes of his managers, who scoffed at his unusual approach to the game.

One manager even threw the books out of the clubhouse. McDowell explained, "The books frightened him because of ignorance — he did not understand it. The books infringed on their territory. Those guys from the 'old school' felt threatened."

Now men such as pitching coach Tom House preach the value of sports psychology and, at one point, John Smoltz even employed his own psychologist. Tolerant managers and coaches now have no problem with a player using any technique to improve his game. Attitudes have obviously improved over baseball's Dark Ages.

As McDowell put it, "Today many players are sophisticated. They read sports psychology books and books on nutrition. There are higher levels of education among the players now."

In fact, after retiring from baseball, McDowell began a company called Triumphs Unlimited. The goal of the company was, as Sam's son and colleague, Tim, said, "Career enhancement, trying to help players get the most out of their ability. Ninety percent of our work is sports psychology, career enhancement, and trying to help players handle any problem."

Over the years the McDowells, pioneers in the field, have truly helped hundreds of players. Sam said that even big-name players such as Todd Stottlemyre, Joe Carter, and Hall of Famer Dave Winfield have benefited from his program. During a 1993 interview, Sam said that Winfield "thinks we have a hell of a program. He didn't even know there was such a thing as we have until this year." Now it would be next to impossible to find any big-leaguer that is unaware of such programs.

He added his belief that players, by the very nature of the game, are vulnerable to an assortment of difficulties. He felt, for instance, that the majority of big-league players have low self-esteem. He said, "They've been taught since they were seven years old that [they're] only important if [they're] winning. [They] get this from [their] parents, from Little League, and from high school coaches."

In *Pen Men*, former star pitcher Johnny Sain contended that many relievers don't actually have the calm nerves they may seem to display. What they do have, he said, is the ability to deal with the pressure. He said he used to play mind games with himself, trying to "minimize the importance" of the game he was about to enter. He'd rationalize that the contest wasn't all that crucial, or, at times, he'd say to himself, "Just see how far you can get today." In other words, he employed the concept of "pitching within yourself."

Matt Mantei, a closer, agreed that players are often insecure. "We really do care what people think about us. We do care what the fans say about us. I think a lot of people don't realize that. Fans think we're just out there and it [the booing and negative comments] goes in one ear and out the other, but it really doesn't. Guys take some things to heart; some guys more than others." Therefore, players' feelings can be fragile and can impact their outings.

With that premise in mind, the McDowells set up a 24-hour service via a toll-free number for their clients. "A pitcher," Sam noted, "who is going to pitch that day might call and want to talk about his concentration skills. He may be experiencing a wildness problem, not because of a problem with his mechanics, but because he can't focus properly."

Tim chimed in, "A lot of our program is based on prevention—for example, with drugs and alcohol abuse. Many of them [minor leaguers] don't make it to the majors due to stress." Sam felt the minor leaguers actually "need us more, yet the major leaguers use us more. In the minors they still view a request for help as a sign of weakness."

Realizing the importance of attitude in baseball, McDowell said he has tried to counsel the temperamental David Wells. But the first step in conquering a problem is to admit the problem exists. McDowell stated, "He's not going to accept any advice."

During each ball game, the pitcher who will start the club's next contest sits in the dugout charting each pitch. The main reason managers have had pitchers do this task over the years is to keep them focused, concentrating on the game and rival hitters. The chore can also help them plan how they'll face certain hitters the next day. To some pitchers, however, it's a task almost tantamount to a teacher assigning "busywork" to a fidgety child.

Cairncross, just the tenth Australian-born player in big-league history, commented, "Every pitcher is different—you can go from a Bartolo [Colon] to a Burbs [David Burba], two different type pitchers. Burbs has a splitter and Bartolo a fastball, but [the pitcher charting a game] can watch the way today's pitcher sets batters up to get to his pitch. You watch how he works the hitter. That gives you an opportunity to see if the guy's going to lunge out and try to pull that pitch or if he's standing up straight. Should I knock him off the plate? It gives you a bit of an idea [how to pitch them]."

As for the actual charts, Cairncross said they record what pitches were thrown—accounting for the types of pitches as well as their number while also tracking which ones were thrown for strikes. Pitchers also are constantly making notations such as how an opposing hitter might chase a pitch with two strikes, or how they should try to throw a certain batter a fastball up with two strikes, or even how a hitter might have a tendency to try to pull the ball, even with a runner on third.

Although it sounds highly technical, Cairncross said, "I think it's really so you're watching the game, so you're not just sitting there b.s.'ing on the bench." After all, he noted, a pitcher who is working the next game should be especially attentive the day before.

Brian Lawrence said the charting really isn't for others to look at, as would be the case of, say, a report by an advance scout. "It's just for us to stay with the game; when you chart it, you gotta pay attention."

After pitching, Lawrence said the length of time it takes for a pitcher's arm to recover from the pain and strain of making a start is "three days. The third day it's usually pretty good. The first day it's not so bad, the second day is probably your worst day, and then the third day you're all right." In a way, then, part of a starter's preparation for his next outing is rest.

Sam Jethroe, who played in both the Negro Leagues and the big leagues, said that what amazed him most about Satchell Paige was the fact that he simply didn't rest—"he pitched three innings or so every day."

Sometimes too much rest can be bad for a pitcher. If, for example, due to rain a pitcher misses a start, he may be rusty and lose his touch and/or control. Often he will be too strong and so throw hard, but not effectively.

Meanwhile Burba, who has started and relieved, addressed his routine. "The day I'm pitching [as a starter for a night game], usually I try to take it easy. Most of the day when my family's in town, I'll get up, I don't know, ten-thirty or eleven o'clock, mill around, maybe do a crossword, take my kids to lunch, come home, relax a little bit, maybe play some PlayStation, and leave for the field about four o'clock." The key word seems to be "relax."

At the park, he continued, "About six o'clock I start getting prepared for the game. I do my stretching, go in and get stretched by the trainer, go out to the field, and start getting loosened up about twenty till seven.

"Usually the night before I'll chart the game and I'll get an idea how I want to pitch them. Then the next day I'll get together with the catcher and we'll talk about how we're going to pitch the hitters, scenarios, weaknesses and their strengths."

As for relying on scouting reports, Burba says, "I like to use my knowledge more than I do an advance scouting report because I don't throw all the pitches that they sometimes [cover]. Sometimes they'll say, 'You can get him out with a slider.' Well, I just started throwing a slider. You can't always go by what their scouting report says because not every pitcher's the same."

In days gone by, pitchers didn't have sophisticated reports—no computer printouts, for example. Many pitchers would actually rely on *The Sporting News* and the daily newspapers' box scores to get information such as who's hot. Burba said such practices are not entirely a thing of the past. Even today, knowing who the torrid hitters of the day are is useful information no matter where one gleans that data.

"A lot of times you'll have a team coming in and they'll have a hot hitter and the pitching coach or the manager will say, 'Don't let this guy be the guy to beat you.' So, you find yourself pitching around him and then the next guy beats you," he laughed. Science, scouting, and study can take a pitcher only so far, but clearly it is best to be as prepared as possible.

By way of comparison and contrast, Lawrence ran down his typical actions prior to taking to the mound. "On game days [for a pitcher's start], you get here later [than normal]. You want to relax a little more and not do anything too strenuous. You might get here and relax, too—some guys might do that. But," he added, as far as the preparation and planning go, "[on] game days, it's over with. If you don't know what you're going to do by that day, then it's too late."

For a typical 7:05 contest, the schedule for Lawrence includes catching the four o'clock team bus to the park. "So," he said, "I get here around four thirty." Thus, for Lawrence, he has a lot of time before he finally heads out to the bullpen to take his pregame warm-up throws.

In late 2002, he said he had yet to study a video of his pitching performances, but he does look over scouting reports. "We have reports that are read every series, and the main thing is I watch [during] the games. I'm pitching the fourth day here," he said of a four-game series versus the Expos, "so I get to see three games against these guys. You've got to pay attention."

Boston catcher Jason Varitek said, "A starter has a warm-up routine, at least a lot of the ones here [do], before they go out onto the field. Then they have some sort of toss program before they get on the [bullpen] mound and throw and then go through anywhere from 20 to, some guys I've heard, 100 pitches.

"It's their own routine of what works best for them," he said, indicating some pitchers will do their pregame preparation with a bullpen coach, the starting catcher, or whoever, but "the pitching coach and the bullpen coach are usually part of it. I go out there. That's the way I get loose, see what kind of stuff they have that day, and sometimes it means a lot, sometimes it means nothing. But at least my legs are [ready] and I'm prepared to do what I'm going to do."

Some catchers will help their pitcher by going over hitters and giving feedback to him prior to the game and, at times, during games. Varitek added, "My job is very complicated in that, yeah, we have to give them our best suggestions." To do this he has to consider "who's on the mound that day, who's at the plate, the scoreboard, et cetera. So, you have to process a lot of information quickly."

Burba also said that when he warms up, "I'll start off [with an emphasis] on just location, not really worrying about how hard I'm throwing, basically we're [working on] mechanics. Then when I get a quarter of the way into it, I'll start breaking out my breaking pitches and start throwing the ball a little harder. By the time I'm at 60 [warm-up throws], the last 10 or so pitches is pretty much a 100 percent."

He knows the right moment when to begin snapping pitches off. "I warm up with my fastball and once I get my arm loose — it's not that I'm throwing 100 percent, but once I feel I'm loose, then I'll start throwing my breaking pitches. Then toward the end of my bullpen [session], I'll throw all the pitches I can 100 percent."

When it comes to pitching out of the bullpen, the preparation is, naturally, different. Burba said he typically uses about 70 pitches to warm up when he's a starter and "maybe 25" as a reliever.

As for his idea of preparation for bullpen work, Scott Stewart agreed with the idea of R & R as he joked, "I just try to relax and shag as few balls as I can during BP."

Stewart, who appears as pleasant as he is relaxed, said he gets to the park for a seven o'clock game "usually around one. I just like to get out here [early]. It takes me, usually, four or five fastballs, two or three curveballs, a couple more fastballs, then a couple of cutters and I should be ready to go. Probably about 10, 12, 14 pitches." The low-maintenance lefty says he does follow the same pattern of the fastballs first and so on.

The cutter, by the way, is a fastball, but it is held with the top two fingers just off center, toward the outside half of the ball. It reacts the opposite of a fastball that tails (in on right-handed hitters if thrown by a righty), and moves only slightly.

Shuey gave his version of pregame preparation: "Commonly, for experienced starters, they'll leave the clubhouse probably about half an hour prior to the start, then maybe stretch out a little bit, do some things. Then they might actually begin throwing 20 minutes prior to the start: long toss and that kind of thing. Then they eventually get in short and get on their program." As for finally really heating up and throwing hard, Shuey stated, "Maybe only, I would bet, at the most 10 minutes."

For the most part, he said, the starters warm up the same as high school pitchers do: throwing their fastballs first then working to the breaking stuff later.

Some pitchers like the last pitch they throw during between-innings warm-ups to be a good, hard fastball, to put them in a groove. If memory serves, Mario Soto was a big proponent of that method. Some amateurs waste their last toss by merely lobbing it toward their catcher—often a high pitch to help them get out of their crouch for their warm-up throw to second.

Stewart said, "I throw all fastballs when I'm warming up in between innings. I don't throw anything else." Likewise, the last pitch he throws before leaving the pen to enter a game is "a four-seam fastball."

Burba said of the necessity of the last pitch being a "serious" one, "I don't know if it's necessarily true. Everybody's different, everybody's an individual, and everybody feels they have their own way of preparing for a game. Personally, I like to end with a fastball because all my pitches work off a fastball. Every pitcher works off a fastball. So I want to make sure that my fastball is prepared and ready to go." If a guy likes to lob the final pitch, well, then "that's just his style."

During contests, a pitcher prepares for each hitter by considering what pitch his catcher is signaling for. When a catcher first starts out, he finds veteran pitchers will often shake him off. Varitek stated, "You have to develop trust. Even now, at the beginning of the year I had to develop that trust with Burkett because he never had that trust in a catcher and now he does in me." Burkett had come to the Red Sox at the start of 2002, so they needed to work out a good pitcher-catcher relationship.

Pitchers also prepare with their catchers a great deal when they're working on a new pitch. Many won't unveil the new wrinkle until they've worked on it extensively during the off-season and have worked (and talked) things out to the point where they have confidence in the pitch. San Diego closer Trevor Hoffman explained his thought process: "I think you're always trying to develop things and it definitely helps to talk to people, but there's no doubt that when you're in a role where the game is on the line [coming out of the bullpen], you need to get people out fast. So you don't want to be experimenting with games on the line."

Cairncross said his method of picking up a new pitch is rather simple. "You just ask the other blokes how to throw it, how they hold it, how to let go of the ball, what sort of rotation you're looking for depending on the pitch, and you just go from there. You experiment—maybe change your arm angle a little bit or try to get a different spin on the ball. You just gotta play around until you master one thing."

Pitchers also vary the amount of pressure they apply to the ball. Further, they will try to change movement by holding the ball another way. Cairncross said he holds the seams differently "depending on what you're looking for. If you're looking for a two-seam, you might want to put pressure on the 'in' [index] finger, off-center the ball, or try no seams. A different arm angle, again, that might help. Turning the ball over might help you, too."

Cairncross said the process takes time. "It's not something you can pick up in a week. It might take you a month or two to pick it up, but you can do it with just a little bit of help from guys on the side—just playing catch."

A pitch to the plate can appear to have a dot on it. This is caused by the spin of the ball making the words written on the ball take on the appearance of a circle. The tighter the spin the smaller the dot looks. A teammate will tell Cairncross how big the dot on the ball seems to be as well as how much the ball "runs" or moves.

From there, the next time-consuming step comes when the pitcher works with a coach. New pitches are perfected, said Dick Pole, the Indians pitching coach in 2000, "in the off-season rather than spring training. Get it started in the winter throwing program."

Cairncross said, "You show the coach and see what he says about the ball—if it's worthwhile [or not], and going to be a quality pitch."

Being able to move up in the minors is often a matter of survival of the fittest. And, in order to be fit, young pitchers often must learn a new pitch. Face it, what gets a pitcher by at one level of the minors may not be enough at the next—just as pitchers are better the higher up one goes in the minors, the hitters improve at each advancing level, too.

Lee Smith said that when coaches consider exactly what a particular pitcher might need to add to his array of pitches, "it depends on the pitches they already throw. We don't like to get kids that throw [both] curveballs *and* sliders because it's hard for the kid to get it in between and start throwing the slurve.

"We [the Giants] have one kid who has a decent curveball, but it's sort of a looping curveball, a lollipop curve, so the guys [hitters] can pick it up real quick. You can get away with it, I mean, he kicked butt; he was like 16–4 in A ball. When he came to Double-A, he got his butt kicked in a league with some good hitters. But he's got a good fastball, so we're teaching him to throw a slider now. When we got him the slider, I think he won 15 games. I tell him to throw more sliders than curveballs. Some guys pick things up quicker than others—it depends on the individual."

Therefore, adding a proper new pitch is a great way for a youngster "to escalate his career," but Smith cautions, "the least amount of change, the better. I was reading this book that said in any sport, a drastic change—such as a guy's batting stance or his pitching mechanics or anything like that—takes about 21 days for the mind to accept that and make it feel normal for him. Well, I say you can get released in 21 days. You screw up for 21 days, you can be shipped home," he said with a hearty laugh.

A great one-two punch for a pitcher can be the fastball and changeup combo. Smith calls this "the best" type of pitching. "It's really easy on your arm, but it takes a good bit out of you to throw a changeup. A lot of guys think that when a pitcher throws a changeup, that it's effortless, but it's just as hard to throw one as a fastball. You try to have the same arm speed as your fastball when you throw a changeup, so what's the difference? It takes the same amount of energy.

"But I think kids get control of the slider a little easier than they do the changeup for keeping the ball down."

At times the positive results with a new pitch come so slowly it becomes a tedious process. Cairncross said, "You might throw 2 good ones out of 30 throws and it's back to the drawing board again—playing catch and experimenting once more." Eventually, the decision might be made to scrap the pitch.

Then again, a pitcher might drop a pitch, only to experiment with it at a later time. Cairncross speculated that after perhaps another year his manager and/or coaches might feel the pitcher still needs a new pitch. Sounding like a commercial for Foster's beer he said, "They might get you to work on a splitty [Australian for split-fingered fastball]. You might be hurtin', so you're looking for a third pitch, so they'll show you how to throw it and you'll battle through spring training."

Of course he noted that the results one gets in spring training mean "something, but not a hell of a lot." Again, it's not something that normally comes overnight, but if a pitcher doesn't give up on, say, learning the splitter, the rewards can be well worth it.

Gaylord Perry, with 314 wins in his career, joked that he had no difficulty learning his version of the splitter (which was really a spitball). "Not when you're 1–6," he said. He learned the pitch out of desperation.

"I learned it from Lindy McDaniel," said the Hall of Famer, "but I learned it from watching, not talking to him about it." On the brink of possible demotion to the minors, and sporting a record that was five games below .500, Perry grasped the pitch with relative ease. He also said, "For some reason it's hard to control for some pitchers, but it is fairly easy to teach the split finger. Each guy who throws it grips it differently."

Former World Series MVP Dave Stewart, a master of the splitter, disagreed with Perry somewhat, saying, "It's not an easy pitch to pick up; it takes a lot of hard work. I learned it during the season with Sandy Koufax."

Shuey said he began throwing his splitter when he was in high school. "Then I kind of canned it for college and just threw fastball, curveball, because it [the split] was a little out of control. Basically, in college, I didn't need anything else. I started throwing harder and the curveball was enough. In high school it was just another pitch to mix in there. I wasn't very developed in high school, so I really didn't know where anything was going, much less [the splitter]."

To refine his split, he got help from "a guy named Tony Arnold, who was a pitching coach in our [Indians] system. [He] told me in the instructional league to throw the crap out of it—throw it as hard as you can and

I did that. I was throwing really hard split-fingers and they were working for me good, so I kept throwing them. I think that's the best way, to get down to an instructional league or to winter ball and work on a pitch—where you can throw it against live hitters and see how they react to it. I got to see their reactions down there to it and [they] weren't real good." So, liking what he saw—batters flailing away—he knew, even way back then at around the age of 23, that this pitch was going to be a big part of his arsenal.

Interestingly, when it did jell for Shuey, he became an unusual split-fingered fastball pitcher in that he threw it so hard. "It seems like most of the guys are able to throw it a little better if they're more consistent with it and not quite throwing it as hard. For whatever reason, for me, if I'm staying back on it at all, it doesn't do as much. So I've got to be real aggressive with it."

Often a pitcher will find success by simply making a slight change, perhaps as simple as dropping his four-seam fastball (which tends to hold a straight course on its flight to the plate but is easy to control) for a two-seam fastball (which dips more and can therefore, for some pitchers, be harder to control). Each pitcher must find what works best for himself. Such tinkering is a part of preparing for each outing.

The use of technological preparation is a given in today's game. Larry Gura, a soft-throwing lefty who won 18 games in 1980, felt part of his success was due to his use of technology, primitive as it was back then. He recorded information on 13 disks (one for each team he faced) to study and analyze opposing hitters. Still, it was a start.

Todd Harris, who manned the radar gun for the Cleveland Indians during the 2002 season, said that a huge benefit of using technology nowadays is "charting upcoming opponents. Our coaching staff will look at the hot and cold zone for opposing batters. Our video department has satellite feeds and we get most major league games. So we're charting an opponent's last five games played to see their trends."

In addition, if a Cleveland pitcher wanted a CD, he "could ask for one of all his curves or all his pitches against a certain batter. It's a tool—you want to make as much available to the players as possible."

Cairncross said that if he had pitched the day before, he finds it beneficial to study charts and videotapes. "I like to see where my pitches were—if I thought they were close. I want to see the action on the ball. Yeah, video's a big thing nowadays. You can pick up a little flaw in your mechanics."

He said when a pitcher is caught up in the game and throws a pitch wide of the plate, he doesn't think about it too much. However, on video he might spot something and say, "Oh, that's what I was doing—I was flying open right there, or my hip was coming out." The fact that a pitcher can watch a given delivery again and again, often in slow motion, certainly helps as well.

Shuey observed that when it comes to the mental prep before the game, entailing the scrutinizing of scouting reports and video in order to glean information on opposing hitters, it becomes an individualized matter. "You get a lot more varied; everybody's a little different, anyway, but some guys like to know a lot and some guys don't want to know anything at all. A guy like Kevin Brown might not want to really know anything about them [opposing hitters]. He knows that he's going to go with his strengths 'cause his strengths are so much better than the normal guy's.

"Then you have other guys who do a lot of studying. I think Finley does a lot of studying and knows what he's got and what he plans to do with a certain guy."

Harris gave an example of how readings from radar guns help to spot trends for a team's pitchers: "For our pitchers, we can instantly see the percentage of strikes they are throwing with each of their pitches. Again, our coaching staff and catchers will notice this and we'll have data to back up their suspicions."

Another benefit of scouting concerns how pitchers might best succeed in attacking enemy hitters. "We see how other teams' pitchers have gone about trying to get batters out," Harris continued. For example, he said, "If they [another club] succeed in pitching inside to a certain hitter, we will try that too. And even if they don't succeed by pitching in on him, we might still try it if our pitcher lives off going inside. In that case, we will try it.

"We never guarantee in our advance scouting report, 'You can get this guy out with inside fastballs,'" he observed. "That guy may have struggled lately but he's still a major league hitter and against us he could be all over it [the inside pitch]."

Harris also said the radar guns are interesting, in that depending upon the angle the gun is aimed at, readings can vary. He pointed out that the radar gun that posts pitching speeds on the scoreboard for fans' enjoyment is often not precise.

The fastest pitcher Harris ever clocked was Bartolo Colon, who once hit 99 mph on his gun. At times, announcers have said the unofficial readings on Colon have indeed hit the 100 mph mark.

Harris also asserted that it's not always easy to get good readings on submarine pitchers. Ideally, he noted, he wants the gun aimed at the pitcher's release point to "get the reading out of his hand. But if a submariner is throwing, you'll get the ball later, more as it comes to the plate—those readings tend to be a little slower."

In addition, some pitchers are difficult to chart for other reasons. Harris recalled, "Kenny Rogers is a tough guy to chart because he throws a lot of changeups to go with his fastballs. He constantly varies his speeds since he's a finesse pitcher, not a power guy.

"Most guys change speeds by throwing fastballs and changeups. Kenny, who doesn't throw hard to begin with, throws a changeup and also varies the speed of his fastball. Jamie Moyer is famous for doing that too."

Harris said that Moyer is, in fact, a classic example of a pitcher who gets by without a blazing fastball, and he has done so since 1986. "Jamie's changeup is a good deal slower than [even that of] Kenny Rogers."

However, Harris says that Moyer isn't as tough to chart as Rogers. Like Moyer, Rogers throws very slowly by big-league standards. Harris said, "Kenny's change is around 81 [mph]. His normal fastball is 85 and the fastball that he takes something off is around 81, 82—it's hard to tell just by the gun readings [which pitch he's throwing] since the speed of his fastball is about the same as his change."

A person charting pitches cannot rely solely on velocity to determine the type of pitch being thrown, but those experts are, of course, highly efficient in determining the pitches as they prepare their reports. Harris explained, "You have to watch the ball as it comes to the plate. Good changeups will fade and sink down and away from righties when thrown by left-handed pitchers."

Harris remembered the time that Rogers had two showdowns with slugger Jim Thome. "In back-to-back at-bats against Thome he struck him out on 89-mile-an-hour fastballs. Later he uncorked a 91-mile-an-hour fastball in a key spot. He can go along in the mid-80s then surprise somebody, getting something extra when he needs it."

One technological trick Tom House employs is to shoot footage of his pitchers at 1,000 frames per second, downloading this onto a computer. Later he can slow the motion down to microseconds to spot problems with incredible accuracy.

Bob Chester, the manager of video operations for the Cleveland Indians, gave his take on how the study of video nowadays can help a pitcher see opponents' tendencies. In order to see how they might want to pitch a guy, Chester said, "what we typically do is have the opposing team's latest games, whether it's to look at the pitcher or their entire lineup, so you can see if they've made any adjustments.

"Say, where a hitter might be standing in the box—whether he's away from the plate or back in the box a little bit. Whether he's striding open or closed, these are all clues as to where they might want to pitch to those players."

As far as specifics go, Chester said that pitchers such as 1988 Cy Young Award winner Orel Hershiser "really looked at his body mechanics. He was definitely a student of the game. I learned a lot from him as far as pitching mechanics and what he looked at for that. We would look at an outing of his and I'd think that he did a pretty good job based on the stats. Then he would point out particular flaws that he saw within his mechanics and was able to try and make corrections."

Studying with (or under) Hershiser actually helped make Chester better at his job when it came to helping other pitchers with the mechanics of the pitching game. Hershiser pointed out aspects of throwing, said Chester, such as illustrating that the "energy that you store is like a spring coiling and then releasing [the pitch] is like releasing the energy and the uncoiling of the spring. Basically [he'd analyze], step-by-step, what he was looking at from the point where he was just standing, looking at the hitter, throughout the entire windup. He wanted to make sure he was doing everything the same way that he typically would do to approach a hitter. He was a perfectionist."

Bob Wickman was an effective reliever for Cleveland. Chester said that Wickman is the type of player to "utilize video more when he feels like he definitely needs to make a correction in his game — if he's having particular problems." In his 2002 interview, Harris added that of the Indians from that era, Wickman was one of those who faithfully used the advance scouting reports as part of his preparation for taking the mound.

Meanwhile, Burba was the type of student who was, said Chester, "highlight oriented. He was, at some point, working with a professional who would help him look at his body mechanics, and Burba would request all of his outings [on video]. He also, like some [other] guys, likes to have positive reinforcement, so we'll occasionally put together a certain highlight tape — for pitchers or hitters [for him]."

Watching tapes of good performances helps to motivate, reinforce positive "behavior," and can instill muscle memory. Therefore, watching a highlight tape isn't an ego issue, but, rather, an effective technological tool for today's athletes.

Chester put it this way: "Face it, baseball is a repetitive sport. Once you've got something down the way you want to have it, it's repetition, repetition, repetition — day in and day out; trying to perform that same stroke or that same action."

There seems to be a definite pattern as to who feels most comfortable with the age of technology. Comedian Larry Miller once said that while his elderly parents were smart, when he purchased a VCR for them and tried to explain how to program it, suddenly a dazed look came over their faces like a deer trapped in a car's headlights. Similarly, in baseball, it is youth who are best served by the age of video.

Ideally, Harris mused, the younger guys on the team can truly gain an advantage through reports and technology, especially those with "computer savvy [who tend to] like it. All of the players look at tape, but some have special requests. If they can gain even a slight advantage, it's worth it."

Chester noted, "A lot of your younger pitchers, and even hitters, are more used to the video-slash-computer age and a lot of these guys will come in and know specifically what they want to look at. Bartolo Colon would come back quite often to look at his outings, but he was looking more at how he was throwing particular pitches, whether or not he thought his breaking ball was working right, the location of the breaking pitch, and also, it's a big part of the game for both pitchers and hitters — where the umpires were calling balls and strikes. Let's face it, when a hitter or a pitcher is in there, they're not only going up against each other, but they also have to make adjustments to where the umpires are calling strikes."

It's not at all uncommon now for a pitcher to request a video or DVD that shows highlights, but only from his most recently finished season. Chester said that some pitchers "might want to just see a certain portion of the lineup [he faced], maybe all the three-four-five hitters."

For the record, DVD use is probably the best route to go for baseball people, much better than watching videotape. Chester explained, "We've found that it's a lot more flexible for the players to be able to utilize rather than having to go to a tape that may have one or two hours' worth of footage on it and have to fast forward and rewind to a particular point. [On DVD], all these segments can be indexed, just like you would have on an audio CD, where they can go to any particular game or situation that they requested, and all they have to do is punch the number and they're there."

Not only do teams use technology to help their pitching staff, they also use psychology. According to Dr. Charles Maher, the sport psychologist and director of psychological services for the Cleveland Indians, about 80 percent of the Indians players have utilized his services. "Some of them [on a basis that's] much more formal," Maher said. "Others are more informal." He helps players in ways such as "testing, counseling, individual plans, consultation with the coaches with the player's permission, . . . anything that the player perceives as relevant to him and his work as a pitcher."

While it's far from being high tech, former Red Sox manager Grady Little once said that the mental part of baseball is very important, especially since "it has a lot to do with your preparation and getting yourself ready for a game, and being able, at this level here in the major leagues, to rebound the next night after a bad night or a good night. You gotta rebound the same way because you gotta play again in 24 hours. So, mentally, if you try to ride the tide up and down, with the good nights and the bad nights, you're going to wear yourself out."

As for the training side of pitchers' lives, most realize their legs provide the drive that helps them push off the rubber. Like a boxer, when the legs go, things turn ugly. Many great fastball pitchers such as Ryan, Seaver, and Colon have had thick, powerful thighs.

Seaver was a proponent of running to build up the legs, and Ryan, at one time a fellow Met, followed suit. In fact, as part of his routine he wore out a pile of stationary bikes, often doing so in workouts after a start. He once hopped on the bike and rode endlessly after he had thrown one of his record seven career no-hitters. Thus, he was unavailable to the media because he refused to vary his approach—not even to commemorate a great accomplishment.

Standout pitching coach Ray Miller endorsed the Seaver-Ryan approach. He felt pitchers who didn't have strong legs would tire in the late innings and begin to throw the ball high—a spot where pitchers invariably get hurt.

Scott Stewart commented, "Yeah, I do think that running's important, but I think more so [are] the legs." He recommends lifting weights to build up the legs and doing "a little cardio [exercise]. As a starter, running is really more important; as a reliever, you don't want to go out and run 40 minutes a day because you have a chance to pitch every day. You do have to have stamina, though." In Stewart's case he says he builds up his stamina just by pitching.

Johnny Sain had his pitchers run, but only in spring training. He felt that once the season began and his crew was going seven, eight, and nine innings, it would be foolish to further wear them out by running them. He said that if the goal of running was to build up strong legs, then his pitchers had proven they were already strong enough when the season began, and their normal work kept them strong.

When he was the Tigers' manager during the Mickey Lolich–Denny McLain era, Mayo Smith once addressed this issue, indicating he wanted the pitchers to run. Sain, his pitching coach, countered by saying that his staff had just come off a league-leading season for complete games without running. Smith was satisfied, and the Tigers continued to defy convention under Sain, who was also famous for coining the phrase, "You don't run the ball across the plate."

Luis Tiant, a standout pitcher, wasn't fond of all the sprints and laps his coaches had made him run over his long career. His logic went a bit further than Sain's great quote when he asked, "How many 20-game seasons has [Olympian] Jesse Owens got?"

When Moyer broke his kneecap in 2000, he decided to give up serious running, sprinting only to get loose before his starts. He began to feel better and even managed to win 20 the following season at the age of 38.

According to the *San Diego Union-Tribune*, Padres closer Trevor Hoffman singled out his father, Ed, calling him a "man of vision." Trevor felt that the fact that he never spent a day on the disabled list was due to his father's influence. From Trevor's days in Little League, Ed had insisted his son throw nothing but fastballs and that he play no position other than shortstop after his Little League days.

So, from the age of 13 until he was 23, "Hoffman never threw off a mound . . . and his first curveball came in 1991, when the Reds converted the Class A shortstop into a reliever," wrote Tom Krasovic.

Trevor continued the story, "In Pony ball, guys wanted me to pitch, but Dad wouldn't let me. I would throw from shortstop. And I think it's a better throw. It's on flat ground, and it's 180 feet across the diamond. So I think I was throwing a better ball than guys throwing off the mound, where their arms were being torn down. I benefited from an extended time of long toss."

Pitchers prepare for the upcoming season at various paces during spring training. Typically, established vets are given leeway as to how they get ready for the opening bell. Ryan said his objective was to increase his leg strength and to log about 30 innings of spring training pitching.

Nagy reflected that the training in general for pitchers is much more sophisticated now than when he broke into the majors. "Nowadays, with all the studies that have gone on, you go around and find a lot more camps, and pitching gurus and whatnot. Every team now has a strength coach.

"When I first came into the league, there was no such thing as a weight room or a strength coach. You just did whatever you did [pretty much on your own], but running has been a part of pitching ever since I can remember. You got to keep your legs in shape, keep 'em strong for a starter, for endurance—that's what carries you through nine innings and 125, 130 pitches, or so.

"And nowadays you incorporate the weights to strengthen your arm, your shoulder, your rotator cuff, and your elbow. You keep your tendons and your ligaments strong. You get into a routine and you stick to it for the whole year."

Shuey said that the size of a pitcher and the bulk of his arm muscle has nothing to do with pitching hard or well. "The only time I ever lifted,

I threw the slowest I've ever thrown," he said. "Most pitchers you find are going to be smaller up top than the rest of the players, because if they do too much upper body [work], they're going to cost themselves miles per hour and late movement [on the ball].

"You try to just keep it nice and thin and limber and lean—basically, just make sure you don't lose that whip. If you lose the whip, you lose it. I don't know of anybody who thinks that pitchers need to be muscle-bound. If you're too big, and there's a few guys out there who are probably real developed and have done things, but I think a lot of those guys have done steroids to get to the point where they're at."

Overall, though, he added, weight lifting "can or can't [be bad for pitchers]. I think there's guys who, when they're on the way out of their career, who maybe get themselves a little boost—that's a little different because you strengthen all the muscles, not just the ones that you see. Usually the ones you see are your biceps and your chest, and those are not two of them that are really good things [to dwell on]."

The prevention of injuries means that conditioning is vital for pitchers. Without it Ryan, for one, would never have lasted as long as he did—he still hummed his fastball in the mid-90s at the age of 46. Maintaining flexibility, for example, is one key for pitchers, and, here again, many experts insist work should be done all year long.

Injuries are inevitable, so now the recovery process is of utmost importance, too. In the old days one way injuries were treated was basically to spit chewing tobacco juice on them and rub. The science of medicine has come a long way. Terry Mulholland told *Baseball Digest,* "There probably are more injuries, but the medical staffs are better able to figure out what's wrong with a pitcher's arm today."

It was a given as recently as the 1960s that a torn ligament or a significant tear in the rotator cuff meant a pitcher's career was through. As for minor injuries, they were inevitable back then and a pitcher was forced to endure them, often pitching through the pain.

Now, rehabilitation techniques help a pitcher along and some even come back stronger than ever before. Likewise, "Tommy John" surgery (elbow ligament replacement) has been a blessing for hurlers.

One-time pitching prospect Jim Wright commented that when he played in the late 1970s and into the 1980s, "There wasn't anything like arthroscopic surgery. If a pitcher went under the knife, they had to cut through so many muscles to get to the damaged area." That, too, could end a career.

Proper training includes diet. House wrote in his book *The Winning Pitcher*, "Eat three hours before the game if possible. The meal should be high in complex carbohydrates." He suggests drinking lots of water between (not at) mealtimes.

Lee Smith had a great work ethic to go along with an even disposition as a reliever. He said with pride, "I knew with me being 6′6″, 240 pounds, I had to work harder than a guy 6′1″, 170. It was going to take more for my body to get in shape, to be where I wanted to be when the season starts. I mean, I didn't carry the game home with me and lose my mind over it, but I know you have to work."

When it comes to training, Glavine, like Smith, is more willing to work than a large majority of pitchers. He feels that if a team decided to go back to using a four-man starting pitching rotation, he and many other pitchers would readjust their conditioning and off-day approach and be able to work with one day's less rest, just as the pitchers of a bygone era did.

Longtime baseball man Jim Riggleman theorized on the switch from four- to five-man rotations, "I think it just gravitated that way as more young pitchers were signed and probably out of the necessity to find a day for them to pitch. You have these young players and fewer ball clubs to put them on as the minor leagues condensed themselves and you've got these pitchers that you need to pitch.

"So they're pitching on every fifth day just so you can see more of your minor league talent pitch. Once they've done that for several years in the minors, now, when they get to the big league, they're kind of programmed to do that. It's kind of a thing that started around the early-mid seventies and it's indoctrinated itself into the game."

One result was the loss of the workhorse pitcher, the guy who threw a slew of innings. "Also the specialization," Riggleman continued. "The game has developed some guys who can finish a game. Even though you might have pitched seven or eight strong innings, you got a guy there who's making three or four million dollars to pitch one inning a day and he wants to show his worth on the club. The manager wants to best utilize him, so he sticks him in there for that last inning or two."

4

Types of Pitches

DURING A 1998 CONTEST, Cincinnati's Dmitri Young swung and missed on three straight pitches from the fireballing Tigers reliever Matt Anderson. The pitches were timed at 99, 99, and 100 mph. As Young returned to the bench he turned to shortstop Barry Larkin and commented, "I wasn't even close on that last one." Larkin grinned. "I got news for you," he said. "You weren't close on any of them."

A dominant fastball can make even a veteran hitter look sick at times. It's also one reason pitchers believe that the first time they face a batter they're in a situation in which, to use the vernacular of tennis, it's "advantage" pitcher. A hitter not only has to worry about timing a "new" fastball, he also has to wonder when it's coming and what other stuff the pitcher has to mix in with it.

Clearly, it all begins with the fastball. When Dave Stewart tossed his 1990 no-hitter, he observed, "If they were going to beat me, they were going to have to beat my number one, my fastball. I used it to set up my off-speed stuff. I was getting the fastball over and when I went to the fork-ball, it worked for me."

Houston pitching coach Burt Hooton stated, "My whole philosophy is that if you don't feed off your fastball you're going to get in trouble no matter what you're throwing." He said that young pitchers who try to retire hitters with breaking stuff wind up in trouble.

So, starting logically with the fastball, here's a look at some of the many weapons pitchers have at their disposal.

The Fastball

Eugene Coleman, who spent time as the director of conditioning for the Astros, stated in *Nolan Ryan's Pitcher's Bible*, "It is ironic that Nolan Ryan can still throw a 95–97 mph fastball at age 43, while less than 7 percent of major league pitchers are capable of throwing 90 mph at all.

"Velocity has decreased in baseball, to some extent, because young pitchers don't throw enough fastballs, pitches per workout, or pitches per week." Coleman contends it takes a great deal of work to learn to throw faster. He said that in Ryan's early days he would typically throw between 160 and a staggering 200 fastballs per outing.

It's true that pitchers continue to establish and work off their fast-balls. Back in 1997, Tom Glavine told *Sports Illustrated*, "If I throw 100 pitches in a game, I'll probably throw as many as 70 fastballs, unless it's a night when I have a great changeup."

In Bob Feller's time, all other pitchers' fastballs were gauged against his. A tremendous compliment was if a pitcher had a fastball "almost" as good as Feller's. Even Ted Williams, who used to brag, "No one can throw a fastball past me," said Feller "was the test." He also said that he'd start preparing for Feller three days before facing him. "I'd sit in my room think-ing and seeing him," said the Splendid Splinter, "thinking about him all that time. God, I loved it. That was a personal challenge."

One of baseball's most famous lines is due to Feller. Lefty Gomez once took three straight pitches for strikes against Feller, unable even to contemplate swinging. As he began to stroll back to his dugout he mut-tered, "That last one sounded a little low."

Then there's a Satchel Paige fastball tale. Hack Wilson once said that Paige's fastball started out "like a baseball and when it gets to the plate it looks like a marble." Paige quipped, "You must be talking about my slow ball. My fastball looks like a fish egg."

Incidentally, while most fans associate the names of Ryan, Feller, or even one of the Johnsons (Randy or Walter) with the fastball, Williams said he saw another pitcher who was the fastest of them all. That man, an obscure name from the past, is Steve Dalkowski. Cal Ripken Sr. wrote in *The Ripken Way* that he felt Dalkowski could light up today's radar guns at around 115 mph despite his almost tiny 5'10", 165-pound frame.

The only problem? The lefty had virtually no control. Ripken Sr. said few people got to see what kind of curve he had because he "was never ahead in the count." One time a Dalkowski pitch got by the catcher, hit the umpire's mask, broke it in three places, and sent the ump to the hospital to be treated for a concussion.

Dalkowski never pitched an inning in the majors and managed a 46–80 record in the minors with a bloated ERA of 5.59. However, he did strike out 1,396 men in just 995 innings. Then again, he issued 1,354 walks, too.

Count Rex Barney as being in, or near, Dalkowski's class. Feller said Barney threw harder than he did. Carl Erskine reminisced, "For the final half of '48 he absolutely overpowered hitters. It was like he was pitching to Little Leaguers. I never saw a pitcher overpower major league hitters like he did then."

Traditional thinking says the bullpen closer should be a man with a dominant fastball, or lately perhaps a wicked split-fingered fastball. During a 1999 interview, reliever Paul Assenmacher said he felt Billy Koch throws about as hard as anyone, calling him the reliever who stands out among the (then) young hard throwers in the game. "I guess he throws anywhere between 95 to 100, but we have Paul Shuey and Steve Karsay who are consistent—up there around 95 to 99." In fact, Karsay has broken the 100 mph barrier on some radar guns. Karsay himself said, "I like Troy Percival's fastball out of the bullpen. As for a young kid, Billy Koch."

Further, it should be noted that as vital a pitch as the fastball is, there is much more to the art of pitching. Dan Warthen, one-time Tigers pitching coach, pointed out, "Major league hitters have no trouble adjusting to velocity. Pitchers have to locate the ball." When Warthen coached for the Padres he noted he "didn't have a guy that blazed it, but the guy who could pitch was Hoffman." In 1998 all Hoffman did was chalk up 53 saves while blowing only one. Warthen sounded like a real estate agent touting the importance of "location, location, location."

Back in 1999, Warthen liked the chances of Matt Anderson, noting that he "is young and coming up. He throws 100 mph and you've got to admire that velocity." He even predicted Anderson would be similar to Koch and become a great pitcher in time. At one point it was written that Anderson experimented with a knuckle-curve and was throwing it harder, at around 90 mph, than many men can throw their finest fastballs.

However, Anderson was sent to Toledo to work on kinks in his mechanics that season. Tigers Hall of Fame broadcaster Ernie Harwell predicted Anderson wouldn't languish there long, and he didn't, but neither has he attained star status, proving once more that throwing 100 mph is no guarantee for greatness.

Still, there is a redeeming feature of a supersonic fastball. As Warthen noted, "It just happens if you throw 95–100 miles an hour, you get by with bad location a little more often."

The nice thing about the fastball is that it's democratic—small men and huge men alike have been known to throw great fastballs. Shuey said that many of the smaller pitchers like Billy Wagner and Pedro Martinez can fire the ball so hard due to several factors. "A lot of it is just arm— you're blessed with an arm that can throw a ball hard. And I would say the biggest thing is being able to create whip in your body, and that has a lot to do with your genetic makeup. There's some stuff you can teach, and there are guys who are up in the big leagues that have been self-taught or taught through coaches to throw harder than they probably ever would have, but for the most part, most of it's God's gift."

To increase speed, he said, "You're looking for torque, to be able to take a baseball and get a whipping sensation that gives it good action late and puts a lot of velocity [on the ball]. You want some action [on the ball] at the end.

"If you look at guys that throw hard, you can almost see most of the guys are in the same position at the same time near the end of the pitch." Shuey said all one has to do is study their release point and "how far they're out toward home plate and how far their actual arm will bend. If you can freeze a camera [shot] and see, most of the guys who throw real hard, their elbow is actually under it."

Picture a snapshot of, say, Koufax, during his delivery—it's almost enough to make one cringe, seeing the grotesque angle of the arm. "You can't even come close to doing that [creating such an odd angle] without throwing a baseball," Shuey added.

When it comes to sheer speed, Clyde Wright said it's a tenuous topic among pitchers. When people asked him how it was that his son, Jaret, threw about 20 mph faster than him, he'd reply, "Well, if I knew, I sure as hell wouldn't be running this pitching school. I'd hire myself out to all 30 major league teams and tell them."

He, too, found it unfathomable that a 6'6" pitcher "breaks his neck" in an attempt to top out around 90 mph or so, while "some little guy that's about 5'8" or 5'9" can throw it 95 with no effort at all."

Feller, a master of the scorching fastball, once said of the mystery of speed, "You can't teach somebody to throw a fastball. It's like trying to teach somebody how to grow hair on a bald head."

The Curveball

Most historians credit Candy Cummings, a man whose name sounded more like a burlesque dancer than a pitcher, with being the creator of the curve, coming up with his innovation in the 1860s. They say Cummings got the idea for the curve when he tossed a clamshell and observed its flight. According to Martin Quigley's *The Crooked Pitch*, Cummings achieved his "best curves by holding the ball towards the end of his fingers 'in a death grip' and, throwing underhand, releasing it with a quick wrist-turn."

At first, the turning of one's wrist was actually a rule violation. Henry Chadwick, however, proposed the legalization of such a move, and by 1872 all deliveries "except overhand pitching and bowling as in cricket" were legit.

There's an old story about a high school pitcher who was talented enough to get offered a pro contract. His first trip away from his small hometown occurred when he traveled to yet another small town with a bush league pro team.

At first the kid does well, feasting on fastballs. Soon, however, the pitchers figure him out, and his average tumbles. Shortly after that, the boy mournfully makes a phone call, saying, "Hey, Mom, I'm coming home—they started throwing curves." There is no doubt, the curve is the great equalizer.

In *The Pitcher*, Nolan Ryan was quoted as saying, "You can't win with one pitch. It doesn't matter how fast you throw." When a man such as Ryan, with his blistering fastball, professes such a point, people listen. In his case, he developed a very effective curve as he matured and became an all-around pitcher.

Catcher A. J. Pierzynski told *USA Today*, "[Barry] Zito gets a lot of fame because his curveball starts high and ends low. A lot of times, it's not a strike, but they call it because the catcher catches it in his glove. But when it crosses the batter, it's still up by your head. It's very hard to swing at."

Having established his unusual curve, he's able to fool hitters more readily. Twins batting coach Scott Ullger said, "Zito gets a lot of outs with his curveball, and then he gets a lot of outs with his high fastballs."

Veteran pitcher Burba spoke of his curve and of some pitching fundamentals concerning how a pitcher holds a curveball. "The tighter you grip the ball, the less velocity you're going to get. The looser the grip, more whip—it frees up your arm. A lot of times when guys try to overthrow, they squeeze the ball and that causes a decrease in velocity." He compared that to the effect of a palm ball, held tightly and deep back in the hand, away from the fingertips. "The tighter you grip the ball, the more tension you have in your arm and the tighter your arm, the more restricted your arm is.

"You can hold it with a looser grip; you can hold it with a tighter grip . . . the tighter, the slower [the curve is]; the looser, the faster." Some pitchers prefer a hard, tight, "shorter break," while others like the opposite. Then there are those who can throw both types of curves.

When a longtime fan thinks of the curve, a few of the names that pop up are Jack Billingham, Koufax, and Erskine, men with curves that curled like popcorn shrimp. Hall of Famer Stan Musial paid Erskine what he called a "left-handed compliment" when he told the Dodger pitcher, "You had the best curve I ever hit. I don't know how I hit it." Still, when it came to a real killer of a curve, they should have called Bert Blyleven's nasty breaking ball "Deadman's Curve," because that lethal pitch put so many hitters away.

Ryan, the king of fastballs, emphasized that his best games, especially the ones with high strikeout totals, were the ones in which his curve, just a few notches beneath Blyleven's, was really working.

As for some of the best in recent years, All-Star second baseman Robbie Alomar said he feels David Wells "has a pretty good curveball," adding he also likes Tom Gordon's breaking ball and Shawn Estes's big curve.

The Slider

Manager Chuck Dressen once said, "A slider is either a fastball with a very small slow break or a curveball with a very small fast break." Either way, Steve Carlton was the capo de capo of this pitch, but it was so easy to learn that scores of pitchers added it to the toolbox of their trade.

None other than Ted Williams said the slider is the best pitch of them all. Closer Sparky Lyle told *Baseball Digest*, "Williams told me the slider was the one pitch he couldn't hit. Ted Williams knew a lot about baseball, and when you hear something from a guy like that, you're going to try to do something about it."

Many other great hitters like Hank Aaron agreed with Williams that it was the toughest pitch for him to hit; plus, it's easy to control. It gives even an ordinary-to-fairly-good pitcher a third or sometimes fourth pitch to puzzle batters—an absolute must to Williams.

Lee Smith agreed that the discovery and use of the slider revolutionized the pitching game. "If you have a good slider," he commented, "it really looks like a fastball until the last second when it gets to the hitting area when it breaks, and it only breaks about six or eight inches. If you throw it too 'big,' they call it a slurve, which is in between a curve and a slider. Then the hitters can pick it up a little earlier, two-thirds of the way to the plate. He knows because he can read that dot [on the ball]." When it breaks tight and late, like Carlton's did, Smith said those six to eight inches are devastating.

Further, the slider in the hands of an already fine pitcher becomes a coup de grâce. Like Spahn, the winningest lefty ever, Carlton always tried to work the corners, never the heart of the plate. The slider allowed him to do just that, throwing a pitch that came down the pipe only to dart outside and nip (or even slightly miss) the corner of the plate.

Longtime Cleveland Indians pitching coach Mel Harder said he always felt that "a fellow with only a fair fastball and curve needs another pitch, and he can usually master the slider." He realized that with a third pitch, opposing hitters would find it almost impossible to sit on a particular pitch.

By the way, Lyle, who had a "pretty good curve" early on, conferred with Williams in 1965 about the slider and bought into the idea that he'd have to develop a good one in order to crash the big-league scene, especially since "I couldn't throw a fastball over the plate." Two years later Lyle's slider was Grade-A, big-league material, earning him a call up to the majors. That pitch helped him carve out a long and productive big-league career.

In the 2002 World Series, Anaheim's Francisco Rodriguez captured the glare of the klieg lights when he displayed his electric right arm and his debilitating slider. His fastball came in at around 95 mph, and then he simply froze hitters with the slider. His actual big-league debut was on September 18, 2002, but he was virtually unheard of until his postseason exploits grabbed attention. He went 0–0 in the regular season, but by the time he had 13 postseason innings in (after Game 2 of the World Series), he had fanned 19 and recorded five wins of the Angels' eight total victories. In all, he struck out 28 batters in just under 19 postseason innings.

The Forkball/Split-Fingered Fastball

If the slider was the pitch of the 1970s, then the splitter became the pitch of the 1980s and beyond.

However, Gaylord Perry said he felt it was ridiculous that the media attached that label to the pitch. His reaction was a sarcastic snort and the comment, "They called it a Cuban forkball back then [during his pitching days] until they stopped getting guys from Cuba who threw it. Then they just called it a forkball."

Former manager Roger Craig disagreed with Perry that the pitches are essentially the same, and infielder Duane Kuiper concurred because many pitchers, he said, "throw it [the splitter] a lot harder than the forkball." Still, it seems safe to say that in various shapes, the two pitches have been around for quite some time, and became increasingly popular.

Plus, whatever one calls it is immaterial; the ball reacts the same basic way. The pitch comes up to the plate appearing to be a fastball. Then, at the last second, if thrown the way a master such as Bruce Sutter did, it drops out of the strike zone and becomes unhittable.

In the book *Pen Men*, Sutter discussed how he took up the splitter. He told author Bob Cairns that coming off an elbow operation, he "was basically afraid to throw the curveball. That's when a Cubs pitching coach [Fred Martin] showed me how to spread my fingers." Had it not been for his injury, he might never have learned his effective new pitch.

Len Barker, who once threw a perfect game, gave credit to Craig, calling him a "good pitching man." He meant, of course, that Craig had a great deal of prowess working with pitchers, specifically as a teacher of the split-fingered fastball. "Before Craig," said Barker, "lots of guys threw it, but he got the best results."

Kuiper said pitchers before Craig's time actually threw more of a forkball than a split-fingered fastball. He added that when men like Detroit's Jack Morris came along, pitchers began to "throw it [the splitter] a lot harder than the forkball." Kuiper also said what made Craig special is, "He doesn't force it on players; if they can't control it, he won't force it on you."

Sutter differed a bit from Barker, stressing that it's a mistake to give Craig credit for the "invention" of the splitter. Sutter said that it was he who actually taught Craig the pitch when Craig was coaching the Padres pitchers. So, he acknowledges the fine work Craig did in passing the knowledge on, but feels Martin deserves the bulk of the recognition and credit.

Martin, by the way, did instruct Sutter to throw the pitch a great deal harder than the forkball and with significant spin to it. Sutter identified his out pitch as being "like a changeup except harder" that caused hitters to get out in front of the pitch because it appeared to be coming in hard. Then, as the batter took a cut at it, the ball dropped.

He said his splitter was different from a straight change, which isn't always a big strikeout pitch. Sutter observed that against changeups, hitters tend to "make contact but [would be] just off a little" leading, perhaps, to a pop-up. Therefore, he concluded, changeups get hit weakly simply because the hitters' timing is off. On the other hand, the splitter was frequently just about untouchable, and therefore led to tons of strikeouts.

Sutter also worked with Cardinals pitching coach Hub Kittle, who called Sutter "the best forkball pitcher who ever pitched." Sutter worked on finger exercises to stay on top of his game, spreading his fingers so far apart it would make the average human recoil in disgust while making a contortionist applaud.

Actually, most experts felt Sutter didn't spread his fingers as much as, say, Elroy Face did, and that's why Sutter gained the label of being a true split-fingered fastball pitcher. Sutter would come over the top with his pitch while having his spread fingers along the top seams. His thumb and ring finger, meanwhile, were gripping the seams under the ball.

Kittle said, "As he comes over and down with very fast arm action, just like his fastball, the ball squirts out with sinker spin from his thumb. The ball comes in looking like a straight fastball with a velocity of around 85 miles an hour. As it gets to the plate, it just seems to sit, like an airplane coming in for a landing."

Face was arguably, and statistically, the greatest relief pitcher ever when based on one season's work. In 1959, Face, with his frustrating forkball, recorded an 18–1 record. When he was asked if he knew which way his forkball would break, he replied, "I don't, but neither does the batter."

In 1972 the Cy Young Award winner was Perry, a man who won more than 300 games and did so with the help of a pitch he sometimes said was a forkball. He won 24 games in 1972 and went on to put together a string of 15 consecutive wins in 1974. He was often accused of throwing an illegal pitch known as the spitball. "The league," Perry joked upon retirement, "will be a little drier now." Clearly, Perry wasn't afraid to joke about his spitball. "I'd always have it [a wet substance] in at least two places, in case the umpires would ask me to wipe one off. I never wanted to be caught out there without anything. It wouldn't be professional," he said, tongue in cheek.

Former Baltimore slugger Boog Powell thought back to his early days as a hitter and said, "Not many pitchers were around with a splitter when I played. But I batted against Elroy Face who threw a forkball; it's a tough pitch. It acts like a splitter; the bottom just comes out of it. It drops like a spitball and you can't tell the difference."

Of course, that is exactly what Perry relied on for years. Once, when asked about his spitball, he stated, "What? You mean the pitch I didn't have?" He insisted for years that his so-called spitball was really just a nasty forkball.

Powell continued his tale of his battle with Face, "He threw it different than many pitchers. Bruce Sutter threw it hard; Face threw soft.

"I was with Los Angeles and I was looking for it," Powell explained, "but it came hard, soft, then softer. I looked bad. It's a tough pitch to hit," he concluded with awe.

Face commented, "I tried to aim it for the middle of the plate and if it got there belt high, it usually sank. If a hitter was looking for the forkball, it made my fastball even more effective.

"If the forkball was working on a particular day, I'd go with it 75 percent of the time. If not, maybe 10 percent."

Face is considered to be the pioneer of this pitch according to former manager Dick Williams, who noted, "Probably some guy threw the forkball before him, but wasn't famous." If Face is the 1950s forkball pioneer, then Sutter became the Neil Armstrong. He was said to throw the pitch 90 percent of the time. Williams said that when Sutter perfected the splitter, it "began the new era of the pitch." Without it, Sutter would've been washed up back in 1978. With it, he went on to reach the 300-save plateau.

Gibson also praised Sutter. "He had good control of it," he said. "If you took it, it would drop out of the zone for a ball, but when you're trying to hit, and the only way to hit is aggressively, you have to go after it. It's easy for an announcer to say, 'Lay off it,' but you can't."

Williams added, "You try to lay off the pitch, but if the pitcher's got a strike on you, he'll keep throwing it."

Tony LaRussa once said he'd take Dave Stewart's splitter over anyone's because he "throws it different ways. He changes speeds and directions," said LaRussa. "He does everything with it." Stewart, though, admitted that it wasn't even his number-one pitch, confessing "it's my second or third pitch depending on the lineup I'm facing."

Perhaps big-league skipper Mike Hargrove, who voted for Morris as possessing the best splitter, summed it up when he said of that deceiving pitch, "If it's easy to teach, it's hard to hit." Stewart called it "not an easy pitch to pick up. It takes a lot of hard work. I learned it during the season with Koufax and worked on it with [pitching coach] Dave Duncan and refined it." He learned it in 1982 but didn't show it until Duncan later gave him the stamp of approval and taught him to change speeds on it.

According to Shuey, who throws a "hard, aggressive" splitter, it is impossible for some men to master it. A pitcher who can't hold the ball correctly simply can't throw that pitch. So Gibson was smart when he said, "I can't spread my fingers that far apart so I didn't mess with it." Of course, Gibson added with his fierce sense of pride, "I didn't need it."

Shuey substantiated Gibson's small fingers theory. "I've got kind of long, skinny fingers and that works well to be able to throw that pitch. If you've got short, stubby fingers like a Bartolo [Colon], I guess you got to just rear back and throw 100 all the time."

Shuey continued, "There's a lot of different grips to help people throw it. I show my grip to most of the guys up here, then they end up finding their own variation off of it. What I like to do is use your two-seamer grip. You take that grip and then you split the ball. That kind of gives you the best indication of whether you're going to be able to throw a split or not. Some guys listen, some guys don't, and some guys do their own thing. [Justin] Speier throws his like a forkball and it's not as hard [as mine], but it's definitely nasty. Guys get here for a reason, and most times they got here by figuring something out. But once they get here, sometimes I will try to help them out and teach them that pitch and see if they can throw it."

When Shuey displayed how he holds his splitter, his fingers were across the seams, not truly with them, with one finger to the right of a seam and another crossing a seam with his thumb "on the front seam of the bottom."

Entering the 21st century, Robbie Alomar said he had a hard time picking the pitcher with the best splitter because "there are so many guys who throw splitters these days. A lot of guys can throw it for strikes; it's a good pitch." Pressed to pick one, he said, "[Roger] Clemens throws one. If he keeps the ball down, it's kind of nasty."

Lee Smith felt the splitter also is revolutionary but can lead a lot of pitchers to pay a visit "to Dr. Andrews's office. It really puts a lot of pressure on the elbow." Smith, having no desire to undergo Tommy John surgery with Dr. Andrews or anyone, avoided the splitter, but did throw a forkball. "A lot of guys fell in love with the thing [the splitter], but if I went in a game and threw 15 pitches, if I threw four forkballs, that would be a lot for me. The split-finger can hurt your arm."

Still, Smith did like his own forkball and would experiment with it. One time when he faced a hitter he just couldn't seem to get out, he threw it with a little less speed and tried to turn it over to act like a screwball. Unhappy with the results, he began to change the position of his thumb on the ball. "If you move it around on the forkball, I used to make it go left to right. Put a little pressure on the inside and it would go away from lefties. Then, when I would throw it to righties, I put [my thumb's pressure] underneath the ball and it would have like a little slider motion to it."

The Changeup

The key to the changeup, also called a change of pace in a different era, is maintaining the same arm speed as is used on a pitcher's fastball. The key to taking speed off the actual delivery is to keep one's fingertips off the seams. It is also vital for the changeup to be about 10–15 mph slower than the pitcher's fastball for it to be its most effective.

Mazzone explained in his book *Pitch Like a Pro* how he teaches the change. "I want you to throw a fastball, whether it's a two-seam or four-seam pitch, and put a little extra on it. Now throw a fastball and don't put the extra [velocity] on it—that's how you learn how to throw the changeup." He added that the trick is to get the proper grip "that will let you throw a fastball without as much velocity." Ideally, that grip would be one's normal, typical fastball grip.

Pitchers hold the ball various ways to "choke it"—that is, in order to prevent the ball from flowing, spinning, and firing out of the hand like a fastball. That's why the circle change and the palm ball work; the ball, when held deep in the hand rather than by the fingertips, will not go as fast.

Of the old-timers, one of the best at fooling hitters' timing with a changeup was Grover Alexander. Later, Stu Miller threw a curve for a changeup and was also the type of pitcher who threw at three speeds: slow, slower, and slowest. While such a pitching strategy may seem suicidal, it can and has worked at the big-league level for more than a few hurlers. So, while experts say you can't continually blow fastballs by big-league hitters, one can fool them quite regularly with slow stuff.

More recently, Doug Jones developed one of the game's greatest changeups. As of late in the 2000 season, Jones ranked twelfth on the all-time save list with just over 300 saves. All that with nothing fast at all. In theory, a pitcher can't last with only a changeup, but Jones pretty much did. One would think that if hitters can catch up to virtually any fastball, then they could gear down and would delight in facing slow, straight stuff. However, Jones changed up off his changeup and befuddled hitters for years.

His change was so effective that in 2000 he whiffed Chan Perry on a pitch that barely exceeded 55 mph. Said Perry, "I never thought I'd strike out on a major league pitch going 58 miles per hour that wasn't a knuckleball. Now I can say that I have."

Grady Little said, "He's got one of those [changeups] that just gets up there and stops on you; it looks like it stops in midair."

The Screwball

Thrown with the opposite twist of the wrist that a pitcher puts on his curve, the screwball may be, on a simple level, just a "reverse curve." But for left-handed hitters who rarely see it, it is a vexing pitch.

Carl Hubbell, believed erroneously to be the first man to throw the screwball, felt hitters had to be looking for the fastball. He commented, "If they're not ready for the fastball, a pitcher will throw it right by them. If they're ready for the fastball and don't get it, they can adjust to the breaking ball. But with a screwball, it isn't the break that fools the hitter, it's the change of speed."

The true pioneer of the pitch may actually be Hub Pruett, a little-known pitcher of the 1920s who had uncommon success against Babe Ruth thanks to his screwball. However, Pruett actually called his pitch a fadeaway, throwing it lefty, but borrowing the basics of the pitch from right-hander Christy Mathewson.

Cobb hated the pitch that broke in on him from a lefty such as Pruett. Once, in a key spot, Pruett, who checked in at a mere 5'10" and 135 pounds, got the best of the superstar and his Tigers. "I got Cobb," said Pruett, "on three straight strikes [all fadeaways], got the next hitter on strikes, and the last one on a fly to the outfield." Cobb, perhaps rationalizing, or merely grousing, said, "That kid won't last long with that crazy pitch."

In a way, he was right. The tough pitch did lead to a sore arm for Pruett from his rookie season on. He was injured when, according to one source, he "made a strikeout pitch, a screwball, to Ruth." However, Pruett did stick around for 211 big-league contests, making life miserable for a handful of lefties such as Ruth.

Regardless of who was the first to throw the pitch, men such as Mike Cuellar, Tug McGraw, and Fernando Valenzuela have since made a living employing the "scroogie" frequently.

The Knuckleball

The French call it "balle papillon," which translates loosely to "butterfly ball." After years of throwing the pitch, and arguably better than any man ever, Phil Niekro would still shake his head, bewildered, and say, "I still don't know why the ball does what it does. And if I don't know where it's going once I throw it, how can the batters know?" That thought was much like the sentiment expressed by hitting coach Charlie Lau, who said, "There are two schools of thought on hitting the knuckleball. Unfortunately, neither of them works."

A knuckleball moves more when it is thrown into the wind. It also works better in high, rather than low, atmospheric conditions. Knuckleball artists, of course, realize that and check on such conditions as soon as they arrive at the park.

From the early part of the twentieth century on, baseball has never experienced a season without at least one man who threw the knuckler. Sources say the first man to throw one was Lew Howard Moren, who broke into the majors in 1904. The next season marked the debut of Eddie Cicotte, sometimes nicknamed "Knuckles," who threw it until the end of the 1920 season, when he was banned from the game due to his involvement in the "Black Sox Scandal," the fixing of the 1919 World Series.

All-Star Travis Fryman once observed, "In my career there's always been one guy, usually an older player, a [Charlie] Hough, the Niekros, and, of course, [Tom] Candiotti, who pitches knuckleballs. Right now there's Tim Wakefield and Steve Sparks." Fryman pointed out it makes sense for an older guy to experiment with the pitch, especially if it's the difference between lingering in the game and leaving it.

However, he noted, "It's a tough pitch to master. The old adage is: 'There's nothing that goes farther than a knuckle that doesn't knuckle.' I think [that] scares some people away from trying [it].

"It's a great pitch," Fryman continued, "very effective to those who have mastered [it]. [But] it certainly has some tremendous downsides as far as wild pitches and inconsistency. It's difficult not only for a catcher to catch, but also for an umpire to see effectively. And weather conditions have a tremendous impact upon the effectiveness of the knuckleball as well. So not everyone's willing to take that chance."

Catcher Tom Lampkin has, over the course of his career, caught knuckleball specialists Dennis Springer, Sparks, and Candiotti. He was asked what knuckleball pitchers do when a hitter tries to adjust to their bread-and-"butterfly" pitch. Some hitters try to move up in the box to catch the pitch before it dips and flutters, or so they hope. Lampkin replied, "If they're knuckleball pitchers, they're going to throw it. They don't care if you're sitting on it; you know they're going to throw it, but it's not a predictable pitch."

And that's the key to the knuckleball: it moves erratically. A hitter can do whatever he wants—move in the box, gear himself up for the pitch, or wear a lucky charm, but it just doesn't matter. Lampkin continued, "The knuckleball pretty much does whatever it [wants to do]. It doesn't come through the air with any rotation, so it's not cutting through the air in a specific pattern. Whatever little pockets of air it hits, it's going to move, which is the reason it's so tough to catch—it doesn't do the same thing every time.

"So, as a pitcher, he knows the hitter knows it's coming, and he just goes ahead and tries to throw it for a strike and lets the ball just kind of do what it wants. Some guys like to throw it a little harder and some guys throw it a little softer depending on what the count is or who the hitter is. Obviously, you don't want to let the guy time it, but if the ball is doing what it's supposed to do, they're not going to hit it anyway. Or they're not going to get good wood on the ball. I don't know if there's really anything to counter it; the pitcher's not going to change his mind anyway. He's going to throw a knuckleball even if everybody in the stadium knows he's going to throw it."

Lampkin feels then that moving, for example, up in the box won't defeat the built-in advantage that the elusive pitch has. "Theoretically, I guess, eventually the ball is going to run out of steam and fall," he said. "It has to. But if I'm a catcher and I see a guy moving up in the box, you can let the pitcher know, 'Hey, he's moving up in the box, you might want to change something.' Or I could tell the pitcher, 'Watch where he's standing in the box, he's moving around.'"

Such a bit of advice could be shared at the end of an inning in the dugout or, if the catcher feels more immediate feedback is important, he can "point to the hitter's feet [during the at-bat] when he's pitching. If I know a pitcher well enough, he knows what I'm talking about when I do that.

"But the knuckleball's the knuckleball and it's tough to counter that. I know some guys who probably have their philosophies or their theories on hitting the knuckleball because they have had success doing it, but I don't know how real that is."

As a rule, it is said that slap hitters, players who stress contact over power, have the most success against knuckleballers. However, it is also accepted that when a knuckleball hangs limply out over the plate, doing nothing, it will be the power hitters who best cash in on the juicy offering.

Case in point: the Pirates of the 1970s had diverse hitters such as Rennie Stennett and Al Oliver who hit line drives and Bob Robertson and

Willie Stargell who hit long, towering home runs. The singles hitters usually didn't strike out that much on the knuckleball, managing to make contact, putting the ball in play while hoping it would find a hole somewhere. Stargell, on the other hand, might fan several times on, say, a wicked Phil Niekro pitch, then crush a few that didn't nose-dive and flitter all over the strike zone.

Experience against the pitch helps a bit. Stennett's first major league at-bat was, in fact, against Niekro, who made him look sick against a diet of knuckleballs. After striking out, a perplexed young Stennett strolled back to the dugout where he was, no doubt, greeted by the old standard, "Welcome to the big leagues, kid."

Hough was still throwing it into his forties, hardly unusual for knuckleball throwers. However, it is a pitch that, again, has its debits. Home runs are, like wild pitches, an occupational risk of knucklers. In a 1989 contest, Hough lost a 7–4 five-hitter; all five hits were homers.

Lampkin said knuckleballs fool hitters also because of their slow speeds. Most big-league hitters love to hit fastballs, not pitches that typically tumble up to the plate at speeds of 65–75 miles per hour. Speeds as low as 58 mph or so are also feasible, he said.

Trevor Hoffman ruminated on the knuckleball pitchers through the ages. "At best, we've seen 50 pitchers who have thrown the knuckleball. Charlie Hough lasted 25 years, which is a credit to him, but for me, it's a pitch that's uncontrollable even to the pitcher."

Still, some pitchers such as Hough, who took to the crazy pitch after he hurt his arm in the minors, have salvaged and/or stretched their careers by learning to throw the junk pitch. Former first baseman Tim Wakefield actually took a career that was dead, went to the minors where he came up with an effective knuckler, and revived his big-league career. Through 2002, he had racked up 105 wins, 21 saves, and 10 years' worth of time in the majors throwing the knuckleball.

The only concessions Wakefield makes to mixing things up is throwing a curve or two along with a rare fastball. Otherwise it's a steady diet of fluttery pitches. As he has pointed out, his pitch relies upon movement, not speed. He holds his knuckler with two fingers but, unlike a few men such as Phil Niekro, his fingertips are off the seams. Like the old joke,

Wakefield says his gauge of how well his knuckleball is working is how clumsy his catcher looks trying to corral it.

Wilbur Wood was a rare portsided knuckler who was willing to take a chance on the pitch, picking it up in 1967 from a master, Hoyt Wilhelm. He also took advantage of the lack of stress the pitch put on his arm. He had a whopping 49 starts in 1972, the first of four consecutive years he led his league in that department, and he logged 290 or more innings in five successive seasons, averaging just over 336 frames per season from 1971 to 1975. In 1972 it was hardly a rarity for him to start on as few as two days' rest, seldom getting the traditional four days off. In fact, over a period of several years he made almost exactly half of his starts on two days' rest, and once in 1973, he started both games of a doubleheader.

For sheer longevity, there was Wilhelm, a 21-year veteran. The George Blanda of baseball lasted until he was 49 years old thanks to the knuckleball. In fact, he worked in 459 games after his fortieth birthday. Not getting his chance in the majors until he was nearing 30, he made up for it by recording 115 saves while appearing in 459 games and chalking up a tiny 2.11 ERA—all after the age of 40. Incidentally, Phil Niekro was still lobbing his famous pitch until he was 48½ years old, and Dutch Leonard lasted until he was approaching 45.

To use another NFL analogy, Wilhelm's knuckleball wobbled like a Billy Kilmer pass. Still, his control of the pitch was remarkable, as he is one of only two knuckleball specialists (who threw it for a significant amount of time) with a strikeout-to-walks ratio better than two-to-one.

Wilhelm said that he learned how to throw the puzzling pitch by looking at pictures, analyzing the grips that former knuckleball pitchers employed. He soon learned that there are various ways to hold the pitch. Some men literally use their knuckles to press up against the ball and push off, while others dig in with their fingernails. In addition, some primarily used two fingers and the thumb while others have used all five fingers in making their delivery.

Wilhelm, according to Martin Quigley's *The Crooked Pitch*, developed two knucklers, a floater and a spinner, using a two-finger grip. He'd place his index and middle fingers on top of the ball, fingernails imbedded into a seam, with his thumb and other two fingers on each side of the ball.

The floater came off a stiff wrist release and had no rotation, while the spinner would break the way he rotated the ball. He said, "I try to make it turn one, sometimes two, times on the way to the plate. It breaks a lot more with two rotations than it does with one. If I release it sidearm, it will break out and laterally away from a right-handed batter. If I come overhand or three-quarters with my motion, it will break down and out."

Wilhelm was helped by often throwing a "soft knuckleball with a three-quarters delivery," allowing him to boast, "I never went on the disabled list, never had a sore arm."

Mike Koplove said sidearm pitchers don't especially discuss their unusual craft with one another to any huge extent. "We've had a few in our [Diamondbacks] pen over the last couple of years," he noted, "but we don't particularly [talk about the pitch]. Once in a while we will, but nothing like we sit there and, 'Hey, how about this and that?' We don't do a lot of talking amongst ourselves about that."

Knuckleball pitchers, on the other hand, have formed strong bonds with one another over the years and are more than willing to share advice. They need to. After all, one thing's for sure: when knuckleball specialists need help, few coaches are able to help out.

When Candiotti had the opportunity to ask Niekro for advice when they both pitched for the Indians, he listed "having Phil Niekro working with me and teaching me the knuckleball" as one of his career highlights. He went so far as to beam, "It was like talking to Thomas Edison about lightbulbs."

In 1960 Wilhelm's catcher, in an effort to box the wildly gyrating pitch, used an oversized mitt. Measuring a gaudy 44 inches in diameter, the glove was banned four years later.

Help for knucklers comes from other sources, too—for instance, most of them tend to their hands with diligence. In his playing days, Candiotti became a sort of amateur manicurist, using Super Glue and an acrylic nail polish to protect his fingernails. Further, nail files are a tool of the trade.

Andres Galarraga has faced his share of knuckleball pitchers, and he, not at all surprisingly, rattled off two names, Phil Niekro and Hough, as the best he had seen. He felt that the pitch was so difficult to hit simply because "it's something different, something you don't see too much. It kind of messes [up] your swing a little."

During an interview in 1992, Padres superstar Tony Gwynn said that he never liked to change his approach to hitting, but admitted that he had to do so somewhat against knuckleball pitchers. Like Galarraga, Gwynn said that facing a knuckleballer could put a hurt on his swing and timing. He said he especially hated facing Candiotti, commenting back in the 1990s, "Every time I've faced him this year I've gone in the tank for three days after seeing his knuckler."

Gwynn pointed out that he geared his swing, normally, to the 80–85 mph range. No wonder he didn't like going up against the slow offerings of, say, Wakefield, who once said that his knuckler was in the Phil Niekro range of 50–70 mph. For that matter, Wakefield also recalled the time a scout clocked one of his meandering pitches at a mere 48 mph. Another source said Niekro had been known to throw his as slow as in the high 30s. Upon hearing that, Gwynn joked, "I'm not geared to that!" It's little wonder then that the knuckleball ruins hitters' timing.

It seems fitting to conclude with Niekro and fitting, too, that Niekro, who baffled hitters for years with his dancing knuckler, was born on April Fool's Day—every time he pitched it was a sick April Fool's joke on miserable hitters. Twenty-six years after his birth he owned zero big-league wins. Amazingly, though, he won 121 contests after he had turned 40. By the way, no other knuckleball pitcher won as many as Niekro's 318, and his brother Joe had the second highest total with 221.

Sidearm/Submarine

Experts say that humans aren't intended to throw overhand, not at the big-league level, not with the intensity and the strain that firing a ball puts on pitchers. Throwing underhanded, or using a submarine style, is easier, more natural. Steve Reed, who throws from down under, said, "It's a normal arm motion. It places less strain on the shoulder than a three-quarters delivery." With so many pitchers coming up with arm injuries, submariners deserve a close look. Reed said that "submarine pitchers can give you an inning or two 70 times a year." And that is very valuable in these days of thin bullpens.

Kent Tekulve spent 2003 as the director of baseball operations for the Washington [Pennsylvania] Wild Things, an independent team. This is the man who set the all-time National League record for games relieved, working in a grueling 1,050 contests. He explained that, other than the actual release point, there is no difference whatsoever between the sidearm style of pitching and the submarine.

"Actually, if you look at video, of myself or any of the guys who threw that way, we're saying that we're throwing submarine, but in reality what we're doing is we're throwing sidearm. We are still throwing sidearm but you lean to the side at the waist. If you stand straight up, you're throwing sidearm, but because we're bending at the waist, the arm angle is down lower. It's kind of like a golf swing; we're swinging down through that area.

"But if you look at the arm from the elbow to the armpit down the side of the body, that's still at 90 degrees just like it would be at sidearm. So, submarine is actually sidearm with a tilt. You physically cannot throw the ball with less than 90 degrees from your elbow to the armpit to your body. You lose all your strength as soon as you do that."

Reed theorized that baseball doesn't have many pitchers who use the down under style because "one of the big problems is that submariners don't light up the radar guns. So many scouts are locked into the radar gun these days." If a pitcher doesn't throw hard, he doesn't get a second look sometimes.

Tekulve picked up on that, saying it's very possible that a talented young submarine pitcher could be overlooked by scouts who are enamored with speed. He opined, "I think scouting has become so technical that it's all stuff that you can enter into a computer. You can enter miles per hour into a computer; movement and stuff like that, you got to put a value on, but you can't just measure it. Plus, I mean, everybody's used to seeing what a three-quarters pitcher or an overhand pitcher looks like. When you look at somebody that throws submarine or sidearm or something that's abnormal, you don't really know what to compare it to."

Arizona sidearmer Koplove said he began throwing that way a long time ago. "I've actually always had kind of a low arm angle to begin with—

it wasn't exactly sidearm, but it's always been a low three-quarters. Actually, the thing that started it, I remember when I was younger watching Kent Tekulve and watching Dan Quisenberry. I'd see highlights of them on *This Week in Baseball*, and I thought it was pretty cool.

"So I'd go out in the backyard and throw like that with my dad and I just got used to it—not throwing submarine style, but dropping down and throwing it sidearm every now and then. As I grew up and continued to pitch, I would always mix that in and it's always just kind of been natural for me to throw from a lower arm angle."

As for the speed of down-under throwers, Tekulve said: "I was probably one of the harder throwers from down there; I threw about 90 [mph] in my heyday. There were other guys that were in the low 80s. [Dan] Quisenberry was about 83, 84 and we both had a lot of success.

"When you throw down there, it's not velocity. You're not throwing the ball by anybody. It's movement and location—that's what you get from throwing down there. So, nobody's ever thrown 97 or 98 from down there—unless it was Eddie Feigner, the softball guy." He was referring to the pitcher of the King and His Court fame, the underhanded (of course) hurler who hit 104 mph on a radar gun, K'd over 140,000 batters, including almost 9,000 while he was blindfolded, and who engineered over 900 no-hitters.

"Because of the movement that's created by the submarine motion, which is the overspin on the ball that causes it to sink, it's a natural sinking action," Tekulve continued. "You don't have to turn the ball over, you just throw it and it sinks because of the way it's coming off your fingers. Because it sinks, and because the release point is down around your knees, it's easy to throw the ball around the hitters' knees, which is where you want to throw it for a sinker."

He contrasted that to overhand pitchers such as "the Nolan Ryans of this world, the guys who throw it overhand and hard. It's easier for them to throw high in the strike zone than it is to throw low because you're letting go of the ball basically on the same plane that you want it to end up at, up high.

"So, in submarine, you're letting go of the ball low and it's actually more difficult to throw it high than it is low. That's because your arm has to go so much further through to the release point to let the ball go [in order to throw high]." Of course, since a cardinal baseball rule is to keep the ball low, "if you keep the sinker down, obviously it's much more effective; it kind of goes hand in hand."

He said some sidearm pitchers might, on certain hitters, try to come up high at times, but he stated, "I think it's a mistake. I think you're always much better pitching to your strength than somebody else's weakness."

For some reason, it seems as if sidearm/submarine pitchers are almost always right-handed. Tekulve said that prior to Mike Myers, who broke in with the Tigers in 1995 (and shortly after that, Sean Runyan, also a Tiger), he could only summon one other lefty to mind. "Ramon Hernandez was with the Pirates [in the 1970s] and kinda threw from the side. I don't think I would call it submarine. He was more of a looping sidearmer, but I don't remember any left-handers [who used the sub style]." He chuckled and added, "It probably has something to do with the rotation of the earth. If you turn a left-hander totally upside down, he's liable to fall over."

Koplove also couldn't recall any lefties who went from the side. He called Myers "the first one that I saw, especially [being] a submariner like that. There might have been a [lefty] 'low guy' before, but Myers is definitely the lowest I've seen. I think it's just something he's comfortable with and he's done it for pretty much his whole career. I don't think he was trying to be the first, it was just something that he had success with, and he's stuck with it since then."

In the 2003 season, Arizona's manager Bob Brenly had a disproportionate number of sidearm pitchers. At one time, he had as many as four men who threw from the side or down under. That included Korean import Byung-Hyun Kim, who was with them from his first day at the big-league level in 1999 into 2003, when he was traded to Boston. The number is upped to five if one counts Bret Prinz who has, according to teammate Koplove, "kind of a lower arm angle, too."

Although Tekulve attributed the unusual amount of sidewinders to coincidence, he did say, "I know for a fact that Brenly, as a [former] hitter, had trouble hitting low sinkerballs. He didn't like them, he liked the ball up in the zone. So maybe he's collecting all kinds of guys that he couldn't hit."

Mark Grace, then with the Diamondbacks, agreed. "I would imagine that we're just trying to go with whoever we can get people out with," he stated. "Kim's gone, but we still have Mike Myers, Mike Koplove, and Eddie Oropesa's kind of out here, too." He indicated a version of a sidearm release. "That's more of a specialist thing. Those are usually guys who come in and get one batter, two batters. You're not going to see many of those type of guys come in for two innings or be set-up guys—they're either closers or one or two hitter guys."

In a 2003 interview, Koplove theorized Brenly had so many sidearmers for a simple reason—because "we've had some good success with it here over the last two, three years. I think he's going to go with whatever's working—if it's guys that throw sidearm, guys that throw overhand, guys that throw underhand, whatever, as long as it gets people out."

Tekulve continued, "Technically, the sinkerball pitchers are all the ones who keep the ball down—although Kim was an example of not doing that. He threw about as many pitches above the belt as he did below. I always personally felt he would be more effective if he just got down around the knees and stayed there, but that wasn't his style; he succeeded in spots."

There are obvious drawbacks to the delivery. Said Grace, as a hitter, "It doesn't take long to get used to that arm slot. It's effective because it's something different—it's a different look. But I'm not a big believer in Byung-Hyun Kim as a starter. I just think that's too many times to see that different angle; I just thought he was a fabulous closer, but I could be wrong."

He wasn't. Before the Fourth of July, Boston, who had acquired Kim as a starter on May 29, announced they were moving him back to his closer role.

In addition, Grace, being a left-handed hitter, recognized that left-handed sidearmers can be tough on lefties. But right-handed sidearmers throwing to lefties is quite another matter. "Myers was never real easy, but most of the right-handers, man, they're giving me a great look at it out there."

Told that Tekulve said he didn't care if lefties salivated over his offerings, that he simply wanted them to put the ball in play, Grace replied, "That's what they're there to do, to get ground balls. Quisenberry, Tekulve, those guys. They put the sink on it, trying to get you to hit the ball on the ground. They're not trying to strike you out; they want you swinging."

Still, Koplove conceded that he, as a righty, doesn't like to let left-handed hitters see much of his sidearm stuff. "I definitely throw from my more natural arm slot against lefties, which is a little bit higher [than sidearm]; for me it's overhand—I think I'm throwing over the top, but everyone that watches me, they're like, 'No, you're still really low.' They can barely tell the difference. It's a little bit lower than three-quarters." He agrees that "from the side, they [lefties] have a tendency to probably see the ball a little bit better [when he sidearms it], so I try to come over the top as much as possible against them."

Tekulve said that baseball's use of sidearmers "seems like it runs in cycles. You'll go for 10 or 15 years where you'll have a couple of guys throwing that way. Then, all of a sudden, they'll go away for a while. After the [Ted] Abernathy era, it kind of died off for a while and didn't show up. And then I came back and Quisenberry was behind me and a couple of more guys were behind us. I was kind of like the rebirth and I didn't do it because it was cool or because it hadn't been done for a while. I did it because I thought I could get people out, which is always the bottom line."

Somewhat unexpectedly, the master of this style has rarely been called in by big-league clubs to help young, aspiring submariners. Tekulve did help a few, including a Mets prospect, but "not too often. I went over to work with three guys in the Dodgers camp one year. I did a contracted deal with them; I came for a week in spring training and worked with the minor league kids. I'm kind of surprised I haven't been called in more over the years with the number of guys who have thrown that way."

As a member of a rather elite group of sidearm/submarine pitchers, Tekulve said he'd be glad to work with pitchers such as Kim if his delivery "got out of whack, but each individual pitching coach and each individual organization has their way of doing things."

He recalled assisting a young Quisenberry. "When I worked with him, there were a whole lot of other people telling him this is what you should do. But Billy Connors [Kansas City's pitching coach then] said, 'Hey, I can tell him all this, but he looks at me and goes, "How the hell do you know? You never did this."' Meanwhile, I was just coming off a World Series. When I told him exactly the same thing [as Connors had told him], he went, 'Oh, great, I'm doing this right.'"

Koplove, who calls himself "more of a standard sidearm" pitcher, has been fortunate in that the coaches he's had, all nonsidearmers, have done all right by him even without firsthand experience with the delivery. "The basics of it are pretty much the same, even the mechanics. I mean, you have to have your arm in the right position; you have to have your release point at the same slot. Obviously there are certain differences, but for the most part it's all kind of the same."

Best Pitches

It's impossible to say who had the best fastball, curve, or what have you, of all time. However, for a sampling from recent days, Fryman listed his picks. "The best knuckleball I saw was probably Charlie Hough's—he had a great one. The best split? You know, I played with Jack Morris, who I think had as good a split-finger as anybody that I ever saw. The young man, Tim Hudson with Oakland, has a good split-finger right now.

"Best pure fastball? As far as velocity, that would be tough—Randy Johnson in his prime, certainly. The best movement on his fastball is Pedro Martinez. I think the best breaking ball is probably Pedro Martinez, and I think the best straight changeup I've ever seen is Pedro Martinez. So, safe to say, I think he's the best pitcher I've ever seen. Slider? I call Pedro's pitch a slider; he doesn't, and David Cone would be a close second in his prime. Pure curveball, probably Mike Mussina, he has a tremendous pure, overhand curveball."

In the meantime, in 2000, Robbie Alomar, who studies pitchers as diligently as anyone, rattled off his short list of the nastiest pitchers in the game. "There's a lot. There's Pedro [Martinez], there's David Wells, there's Randy Johnson and Greg Maddux." With an obvious understatement, he concluded, "They've got good stuff."

5

Attitude and Confidence Factors

A PITCHER'S ATTITUDE and mental outlook on the game can be crucial. Confidence may be the most important attitude to carry into a game. Before exploring that, here are some other facets pertaining to other attitudes in general.

Big-leaguers realize that if there is something that annoys or distracts them, they should avoid or eradicate that issue. Some pitchers such as Roger Clemens have displayed an aversion to having the speed of their pitches registered on the scoreboard. His solution was simple, at least when pitching at home. He instructed the scoreboard operators to quit displaying the speeds of his pitches.

Shuey, on the other hand, said, "It's fine with me. My whole deal is that I've never looked up there; not once. A lot of times, though, you get young guys who come up there and they're looking up there after every pitch. It can be a distraction for some people.

"I know that my job is to just get people out and it's not to throw hard or to do this or to do that. Basically, if I just get those guys out, nobody really cares about anything else that I do. I don't pay attention [to the speed display]. Afterwards, my dad might tell me, 'You were throwing this [speed].' Afterwards, I might want to know, but when I'm doing it, I'm focusing in on that catcher—that's all I'm looking at."

He did admit that he has learned that he's "hit a 100 a couple of times. It hasn't been often, it hasn't been a lot, but I've hit it. This year, since I got past the hip surgery, I think the highest I've gotten is 97. That's *all right*," he conceded, "but I think last year around this time I was doing a little better, being more consistently hard. This year I have had some days when I haven't been able to push that well [off the rubber] and the speeds have really dropped off, but you just keep going out there making your pitches and good things will happen."

The proof that pitchers such as Shuey may not be obsessed about their speeds, but that they are interested, came when he commented on his breaking the 100 mph barrier, "I feel great about it," he said. "I like it. If there was a 'club,' I'm in it and I feel good about it."

Billy Koch is one reliever not obsessed with stats. In August of 2002 he racked up his thirtieth save for the fourth straight season. In a postgame interview he commented, "I never set a number on how many saves I want to get because that feels like a limitation."

In a somewhat similar scenario, Tim Hudson said the A's starting staff had the attitude that they want to excel, to reach their personal best, while feeling that there are no limitations on what they can achieve. That, he believed, creates a sort of friendly competition. "You don't want to be the weakest link of the pitching staff, so you bust your behind and keep up," he said.

All pitchers love it when they're in the groove. To be able to simply throw the ball, knowing that you're in a rare "zone" when everything you throw is going to go where you want it to go, is as delightful as it is rare for many hurlers. Right-hander Jamie Brewington said that pitchers "feel it" when they're in the groove, not unlike a hitter who is the midst of a hot streak. "It's almost where you feel 'I can't do any wrong.' You pick your spot and throw to it."

When San Francisco had both Rod Beck and Robb Nen in their bullpen, they were blessed with two great arms, but, at that time, Beck was considered the closer. However, one day the Giants manager decided to let Nen work the ninth inning in an easy save situation. He made the move to save Beck's arm a bit, but wound up making Beck furious. Closers not only want the ball, they also tend to fuss about their skills a great deal. Further, since statistics are used to measure those skills, most closers care dearly about their saves. Beck wanted the work and he definitely wanted the save, even (perhaps especially) an easy one.

Billy Wagner said he understands such thinking, commenting, "You got so many one-run pressure games, you're in that pressure cooker, and you get through it and convert those saves. But sometimes you get that three-run lead—that, to a closer, is the easiest [save] you can get because you can go out there and make some mistakes, give up some runs, and still get a save. In my opinion, the closer should be rewarded for all those times going out there when [it was tough]. It's a gift from the team and from your manager."

Lee Smith added, "I think closers get into the situation where they come into the ballpark knowing what their job is. If you go to work tomorrow and somebody's doing your job, you wouldn't be very happy. But I think it makes the team stronger to have two guys they can go to in a [tough] situation.

"I didn't mind at all when a young guy was coming in. When I was in Anaheim, we had Troy Percival, and I helped him as much as I could. The guys were like, 'Hey, man, you're teaching the kid to take your job.'

"I said, 'This guy's throwing 100 miles an hour; he's going to have a closer role somewhere.' I just felt it made me a better person, trying to help someone because I know somebody helped me when I came up.

"Some of the guys get a little selfish, though, in situations like [the Beck scenario]. But I think you find so many guys get better when they come to the ballpark and they know where they're going to be used."

In 2003 a similar occurrence to the Beck controversy took place when White Sox closer Koch held a ninth-inning, two-run lead, just one out away from registering another save, but with two men aboard. Manager Jerry Manuel called to the pen for a lefty who got the save. Koch fumed, tossing his glove into the stands as he neared the dugout on his departure from the game.

After a private meeting, things calmed down and Manuel told the media, "Billy Koch is the guy who wants to be out there when the game is on the line. He's like that guy Vin Diesel—he drives on the edge all the time. I just don't want to be in the car with him at the time."

Saves are precious, to be sure. Sometimes a save in, say, a three-run lead situation is not as much of a breeze as it may seem. Some relievers aren't accustomed to working with such a margin of safety, and Wagner says that may lead to the pitcher relaxing somewhat on the mound. "It's a gift, but it's also one of those, 'Oh, my gosh, it's a three-run lead. What'll I do? I've got room for a mistake' [things].

"A lot of times that's tougher because you *know* you have that room, so you don't go out there and pitch as fine and with the same intensity [as usual]. Next thing you know, you give up a hit, another hit, and now you've got the tying run up and you gotta bear down, and that's really tough."

Next, there's the makeup of rugged Randy Johnson, whose attitude about the game was a legacy from his father. Johnson, who, by the way, stood 6'8" when he was in high school (another legacy), stated that his father taught him to make the most of every opportunity in life. "You have an opportunity to throw that pitch one time. To pitch in that game one time. Those 'one times' have come into play a lot for me in my career. I draw strength from him."

Another lesson Johnson gained from his father was not to be complacent, that there is always room for improvement. "He was the disciplinarian in our house and he instilled discipline in me." Even after Johnson's no-hitter, when he called his father from the clubhouse and told him what he had just done, his dad asked how many walks Randy had surrendered.

At times a starting pitcher (though usually not the ace) who is getting shelled unmercifully will be called upon to absorb more punishment to his ego and his earned run average by continuing to toil. This commonly happens if his team's bullpen is depleted and needs a rest.

Shuey stated, "You're expected to do that. It doesn't matter who you are. They may protect some people, but when they're protecting people it's more like a big star who might be a little more fragile and he's going to be a lot better if his confidence is high. They know if his confidence gets down, he's not going to be as good, so I think there's some protection that way; but for the most part, it's a business and the guys are going to use you to the best end of their business. If that means suck it up—105 pitches in three innings—then that's what you're going to do."

Shuey added that even though a pitcher is expected to struggle through such a shellacking, he's simply being a professional about his job when he becomes a scapegoat, and it is appreciated by management and fellow teammates alike. It's the old "take one for the team" concept applied to pitchers.

Bob Brenly said that self-sacrifice is not only expected of a pitcher, but that most players are not selfish and would think of their team first. There was the case of starting pitcher Jamie Moyer, who got a start once during a stretch when his team's relief corps had been badly overworked and therefore desperately needed rest.

He took to the mound thinking he had to give his team seven innings or so. Instead, he got ripped from the outset of the game. Realizing his team was probably going to lose anyway, he sucked it up, stuck it out for well over 100 pitches, and suffered through a beating.

Brenly, recalling Moyer's great team attitude, added, "There's a lot more of [such sacrificing] than you would imagine. I don't know if I could put a percentage on it, but I've been around this game a long time and the guys who care more about their stats than their team winning are definitely in a minority—a small minority."

Men such as Clyde Wright hated to miss a turn on the hill. He once said, "I know when I was playing, if I missed a turn, oh, I'd just get ill—bite somebody's head off." He resented coaches telling him a missed start was for his own good, since Wright felt he knew his own body better than anyone.

When Charlie Manuel was the Indians' manager, he said that one definition of what managers want in a pitcher is simple. "I like the guy who seems like he can pitch and win when he doesn't have his good stuff. He'll battle through. We got some guys on our team like that—Chuck Finley's that way and so is Dave Burba.

"It seems like on days they do not have good command, they don't have their good stuff, they can get you through six or seven innings."

As would be expected, Hoffman relishes the role of being the "go to" guy out of the pen. When it gets to the stage that he enters a game, it's usually a case of his being the last line of defense—it's in his hands. "I think it's important to know you don't have a lot of outside factors you're going to have to worry about," Hoffman said. "When roles are defined, with everybody, not just a closer, [it's important]. If your starting pitching's good, you're going to go deep in the ball game—that allows your bullpen to set up and know that someone's got the sixth inning, someone's got the seventh inning, someone's got the eighth, and you've got your closer.

"And if your [starting] pitcher goes further, then you just bypass those first couple of steps and guys know where they fit in. There's no doubt that guys are successful when they don't have to be looking over their shoulder."

Big-league pitchers really do pack a lot of pride into their uniforms. Many even fret over their statistics with almost maternal care. While some statistics are relatively meaningless to players, Lee Smith said, "Inherited runners was one of my main peeves that I had—it was a stat that I really wanted to watch. I had this thing about wanting to be the best on the team at that. I *hated* giving up a teammate's run. I'd rather give up ten of my runs than one of my teammate's.

"You know you're being a good relief pitcher if your inherited runners [who wind up scoring are kept] down. You want to get the first out and, plus, most of the time when I came in, before I was *the* closer, I was pitching in the seventh and eighth inning and there would always be somebody on base. If you don't get that guy there, there's no save opportunity."

Wagner spoke of how demanding the mental side of the game is. He said having to be able to throw a payoff pitch to a threat such as Mark McGwire is a strain. Further, it's a strain that closers have to face, by the very nature of their role, night in and night out.

Sadly, there are some pitchers who go into an abyss, losing their ability to pitch, and never regain it. From 1968 to 1972 Steve Blass won 18, 16, 10, 15, and 19 contests. In 1973, however, he simply fell apart. At 31 years of age, and coming off a 19–8 (2.49) season, he went 3–9 (9.85). The following year he worked one game for five innings, five hits, five runs, and a telltale seven walks. After that, he was through for good. To Pirate fans the "disappearance" of his control and effectiveness was as inexplicable and as puzzling as the vanishing of Amelia Earhart or Judge Crater.

Gene Clines was a teammate of Blass's in Pittsburgh. His recollections of the one-time star pitcher were all positive. "He never changed. He was always the same guy in the clubhouse. He kept it loose. He was your practical joker, the agitator—even when he was in a slump."

For Mark Wohlers, another pitcher who suddenly lost his skills, the situation was a bit different in that, unlike Blass, he did salvage his career. But clearly Wohlers was never as dominating as he had once been. As of June 2003, a bleak jury was still out on Rick Ankiel of the Cardinals, while it appeared another pitcher whose problems were rooted in control difficulties and/or a mental block, John Rocker, was finished when the Tampa Bay organization cut him.

It's understandable that a pitcher may have a problem putting the ball where he wants at the speed he wants. Believe it or not, though, a big-league pitcher once even had trouble when issuing an intentional walk. All-star catcher Sandy Alomar Jr. told the story of Eric Plunk and his woes. "Sometimes you cannot throw at in-between speeds. Guys who throw 90 can't throw the ball at 60 unless they lob it."

So, what should be one of four safe, wide ones can wind up being a very wild pitch. "Plunk did it one time," Alomar explained. "He threw a ball way over my head." Alomar Jr. likened it to the times a pitcher fields a come-backer and aims a soft toss to the first baseman only to see it soar wildly down the line. Clearly, putting the ball where one wants to is no easy task.

In fact, pitcher Steve Woodard said it's very difficult to throw strikes *effectively*. "It's one of the hardest things to do. One of the other hardest things to do is hit a baseball, so it's a tough game. A lot of people don't understand and realize that there are situations where you don't want to throw a strike; you don't want to throw it down the middle and let a guy hit it."

Before a pitcher earns a reputation and the right not to fret about his manager yanking him from a game, it's only natural for a pitcher to have self-doubts or fears. Hoffman candidly admitted, "I don't think something like that ever really goes away. I think you have confidence in yourself, but there's always a sense of negativity that creeps in your head, that you have to address and flush out with some positive thoughts.

"I don't care if you're one day in the big leagues or ten years, you're going to have doubt in your ability at times," Hoffman continued. "It's just how you handle that and know that your stuff *is* good enough to keep getting guys out. The ability to do that is being effective and visualizing quality pitches."

Was there, though, a moment in Hoffman's career (and by extension, in any good pitcher's career) where he felt, "I'm here to stay; I can get these guys out"? Hoffman insisted he doesn't tend to think like that. "Personally, I don't look at my situation in any type of sectors. I think I came up with the same mentality I use now, and that's I concentrate on one pitch at a time, that turns into one out at a time, that turns into one inning at a time, one year at a time—there are stepping stones.

"I don't think you can get to any particular point of success by looking too far in advance. If you think: keep things simple and control the one thing that you can control, and that's that particular pitch at that moment, then you can live with it."

When Matt Mantei was struggling a bit back in July of 2000, he stated that one aspect of pitching that he hated is failure. "I think more than anything else, we have an emotional roller coaster," Mantei said. "Everybody wants to succeed every time they're out there, and you know that's not going to happen. You got to learn how to go through the ups and downs."

Woodard concurred. "Baseball is a game of failure," he said. "The best hitters go out and get themselves out 7 times out of 10 at-bats. As a pitcher you've just got to go out every day and give it 100 percent. It may not fall your way one day, but the next time you go out, it may."

To lack confidence completely is to fail. Directly out of high school, David Clyde broke into the majors with a sensational smash, at least publicity-wise. He soon floundered, though, and wound up with 18 career wins. He scrutinized the reason why, saying, "Instead of believing in my abilities, I thought, 'I'm throwing 95 miles an hour, or whatever, now I've got to throw 100.'

"Every time I failed, I thought, 'Damn, I've got to get better.' Doubts started to creep in." And that, basically, was that for a once-promising career.

Another take on the subject came from Nagy, who stated, "The biggest mental hurdle you get over when you first get called up to the big leagues is just that feeling of you belong and that you're part of this team, and, 'Hey, I can pitch here.' [It's] the confidence that you can get the other guys out. I mean, you come up and you're just in awe and you look around at the big names, the guys you read about in the paper and you hear about on *SportsCenter* all the time. You don't know whether to throw them a strike or to get their autograph. So that's the biggest hurdle that you have to get over."

It may seem hard to believe for most baseball fans, but big-leaguers do get jittery. Jason Varitek said he's known closers, for example, who get that butterfly feeling, but "I think that's what makes them good—they're still able to use that adrenaline each time they go out there."

He's even seen cases, in big games, where a pitcher became too pumped up, which can lead to overthrowing the ball at times. "I had my first playoff experience with a guy that had 14 years in the big leagues, [Tom] Flash Gordon, and it was the first time he pitched in the playoffs, so he was a little jacked up and a little nervous. Once you get through that, then you go back to playing the game."

It's much like what pro football players say they experience before a Super Bowl—they are nervous until they make their first physical contact with an opponent. Then they settle down and their skills and experience take over.

Some pitchers don't seem to have, or at least don't outwardly display, any nerves on the mound. They exude confidence to the point of being accused of being cocky, arrogant.

During a 1997 interview, Atlanta's Chipper Jones said he considered, along those lines, one of the most colorful pitchers in the game to be "Carlos Perez, who dances around the mound much like his brother Pascual did with the Braves awhile back. He makes a lot of people mad, but he puts butts in the seats and that's what people like nowadays."

While Jones went as far as to label Carlos "quite a character," Jones felt Carlos's attitude on the mound wasn't harmful. He said, "Oh, he's flaky. *Definitely* flaky. But I know Carlos on a personal level, and he's very colorful, happy-go-lucky, and he enjoys playing the game. I don't think he does [his gyrations] to show anybody up, he's just out there having fun." And, as most anybody in the game will say, players have to be loose to succeed in baseball.

However, the line between staying loose and being a hot dog to the point of harming one's performance is a tenuous one. If a pitcher, for example, crosses over that line, it's not at all unusual for a teammate such as a veteran leader to have a sort of father-son talk with the pitcher, pulling him aside to teach him the baseball facts of life. As former manager Terry Collins put it, "When your teammates start saying, 'Hey, a little of that [clowning] is OK, but . . .'" an ultimatum is implied and usually clearly understood.

Collins went on to say, "Even Carlos Perez [has learned what's acceptable]. When I was with Houston we would play the Expos and he would pitch. All he did [with his antics] was fire up the other team. He got them angry. We had pretty good success against him because our guys wanted to beat him."

House, author of *The Winning Pitcher*, subscribes to the self-fulfilling prophecy, which states if a player feels he can't succeed, he won't. He wrote, "Negative thoughts about what could happen stops them [pitchers] from achieving maximum performance. It's strange because, when asked up front, few players are afraid to go out and pitch. What they fear is how they will feel after they have gone out to pitch." In other words, a pitcher harms himself by worrying about something negative that hasn't even happened yet—and perhaps *wouldn't* happen if the pitcher didn't have what House equates to a fear of failure, similar to stage fright.

Such mental aspects of the mound have been studied in depth. Bob Chester of the Indians' video department said that his tapes aren't just studied by players and coaches. Baseball has become so specialized that even the team director of psychology will take a look at players on video.

Chester pointed out, "A lot of times we'll prepare tapes for those guys based on what a player does. Say a pitcher who gives up a home run—they'll look at how he handles that. If a player's shoulders drop or whatever, or they blow their cool, that's all signs to the opposing team that, 'We're getting to this guy.'"

The player who is displaying, as they call it in poker, a "tell," a tip-off that he's losing his stuff and/or confidence, can work on that formerly seldom-considered psychological phase of his game.

One way Dr. Maher gets detailed feedback about a player is by observing his body language, often by studying video. "It's an indicator of composure, of confidence, of focus, and of discipline."

Along with observation comes analysis. Maher said, "The video is used for pitchers to identify what they're doing well and also to pinpoint things that they are not doing well, that they need to improve on. It's all based on an individual plan and knowing the level the pitcher is at, whether it's major league, A ball, or Double-A."

However, in a sample scenario, a young pitcher approaches Dr. Maher asking for help. After rapport is built up, he can try to help the player, say, buoy his self-esteem and improve his performance. For this purpose Dr. Maher has developed a mental skills checklist that includes 12 mental domains that are important to the player's success—things such as confidence, focus, emotional intensity, and communication.

The doctor and player would watch video and the pitcher "would observe himself, so that he could describe himself as he sees himself, and then try to relate that to some feelings or mental state that he was going through at the time. Then, using that as a basis for discussion, possibly change certain habits or certain routines that he might have.

"If I were asked what's the most important thing for professional athletes to have," Dr. Maher said, "it's the awareness of themselves— awareness of what they do well and why, and an awareness of what they're not doing well, and what might be the reason."

So, when dealing with those players who have a short fuse or who lack confidence—perhaps a pitcher who surrenders a home run, then loses his cool and tries, perhaps, to overthrow—the question is this: can such a basic personality trait be altered or at least harnessed?

Dr. Maher responded, "What you're changing is their ability to iden-tify the situations when they will become frustrated, lose their temper, and then work on changing particular thoughts and behaviors to go along with that. In particular, helping them to recognize situations where they are likely to lose focus and intensity and engage in an activity like deep breathing, stepping back, centering himself, getting back into the moment, and throwing the next pitch for a quality pitch."

The next time you see a pitcher give up a gopher ball, watch his reac-tion. Many players into the mental side of the game will indeed react as Dr. Maher pointed out. Such getting-back-on-task maneuvers are much more productive than getting so angry they groove a fastball, or, as the doctor put it, "letting your emotions take you out of the game."

Anaheim's Jarrod Washburn admitted his pregame confidence isn't exactly silky smooth. "But when I pitch," he stated, "once I face that first batter, the nerves are gone." Jorge Fabregas, who has caught him, said, "He doesn't have the greatest stuff in the world, but he'll challenge you. He'll say, 'Here's what I got, let's see what you can do with it.'" He even went right at Barry Bonds in the 2002 World Series. When Bonds hom-ered, Washburn simply smiled it off.

The origin of a player's confidence may stem from various factors. Sometimes it's based on past performances against a given hitter. If a pitcher has held a decided advantage against a hitter over a period of time long enough to establish a track record, then when he again faces that man, the pitcher *believes* he will get him out. That attitude and advantage is impossible to measure, but it is obviously a big plus. It's the flip side of the "I know I *can't* do it" self-fulfilling prophecy.

At times the "why" of a pitcher's luck over a hitter is simply inexplicable—even the pitcher doesn't know why he's getting the guy out. Seldom does he care; he just wants that success to keep on rolling.

Good control can breed confidence. Grady Little was asked how many times out of 10 a major league pitcher throwing on the side with his catcher could hit his mitt. Little replied, "A guy like Greg Maddux could hit it 11 out of 10 times and it doesn't matter if a hitter's in there or not.

"That's the biggest difference between major league pitchers and pitchers coming up," Little added. "Or amateur pitchers—location of their stuff. Not how hard they throw it, but where they can put the ball and how often they can do that."

Little went so far as to say that he feels a typical major league pitcher, when it's vital *not* to miss the location he wants to hit "in a game, [he'll hit it] probably 80 percent of the time." And if he doesn't hit his spots that often, he may soon find himself with a bloated ERA or with a packed suitcase, headed back to the minors, self-confidence shot.

When it comes to displaying confidence, at times ostentatiously, Curt Schilling is a veritable carnival barker. His pitching ability draws crowds to his thrilling sideshow—like the time in an All-Star game when he faced Alex Rodriguez. As A-Rod stepped in, Schilling offered up a friendly challenge: my best against yours. He actually told Rodriguez that he was going to throw "nothing but fastballs" and proceeded to whiff him.

Early Wynn not only oozed confidence and a feral quality on the mound, he had an unmatched determination. Wynn's ex-roommate, Jerry Walker, said, "He didn't like to lose—ever!"

In order to help his chances of winning, Wynn even learned how to switch-hit. And when it came to his shot at reaching the magical 300-win plateau, he was not to be denied. It took the 43-year-old Wynn eight starts, but if necessary he would have lingered forever, seeking that 300th win. As he put it when asked when he would retire, "Somebody will have to come and tear the uniform off me, and the guy who comes better have help."

Dean Chance, a pitcher who had an ego that matched his confidence level, won the Cy Young Award and did so, if he is to be taken literally, using his ego along with "eight different pitches, including a snakeball, a super snakeball, and a one-pronged forkball. You can call your story 'The Farm Boy Makes Good,'" he told a writer.

Even as a youngster, Steve Carlton owned an uncanny amount of genuine confidence in himself, which bordered on being brash. A story has it that after his first game as a Cardinal, he called veteran catcher Tim McCarver aside and informed him, "You've got to call for more breaking pitches when I'm behind in the count."

Carlton was wise to do what he did according to House, who said a pitcher must be the guy who takes charge, who makes the decision as to what pitch to go with. He said, "Throw what you want to throw—if you can't decide what to throw, step off the mound and start over. The wrong pitch that you believe in is better than the right pitch thrown with less than total commitment."

One reliever who also was fearless and highly self-assured was Dennis Eckersley. Even when undergoing a bad stretch, he said he would "try to fake my way through it sometimes. You talk yourself into acting like you got it going on again. But deep down, you know you don't. If you wait long enough, things always turn around."

Pitching coach Mark Wiley spoke of the closers' mentality, saying when they are throwing well they feel things will somehow work out well. Even when a great closer makes a poor pitch, Wiley said he will "still come out smelling like a rose. He hangs a pitch and the batter lines on right at the shortstop. The pitcher just knows that something good is going to happen. As a pitcher, you have to visualize the [intended] result." It's almost as if his confidence allows him to telepathically guide the ball, to *will* the ball into a defender's glove.

Arizona closer Mantei said, "I don't like hitters. I try not to even talk to them. I don't care if it's Ken Griffey Jr. or somebody that just got called up. To me, they're all the same."

His one-time pitching coach, Mark Connor, touted Mantei's attitude. "He has that determination, the fire and confidence to be a closer. He's got that closer's mentality, you know, 'Take no prisoners.'"

When John Smoltz, after many years as a successful starter, became a closer, he told *Sports Illustrated* that he wanted to have a mantle of invincibility, a closer's most important strength. "You want that aura so that the other team thinks, 'Uh-oh, if they have the lead in the ninth inning, we're in trouble.' You want them to think that when you walk in, that game's as good as over."

6

Pitching Tips and Techniques

AN OLD BASEBALL line says that the most important pitch in baseball is
"strike one." It is the pitch that, if thrown right away, puts the pitcher in
the driver's seat and sets up his entire sequence for that confrontation.
When a hitter is down 0-1, a pitcher is in good shape to really pin him
down at 0-2 with a good second pitch. Jumping on top in the count and
staying ahead of hitters is reminiscent of an old line Ray Miller used to
preach, "Throw strikes, change speeds, and work fast."

It all makes sense, especially since a statistical study showed that
when a batter swings at the first strike, the percentage of base hits coming off strike one is lower than on any other pitch. In fact, the study
showed that hitters are most likely to either take the pitch, foul it off, or,
when they do put it in play, make an out.

An effective pitcher must have more than a sizzling fastball—even
a Randy Johnson–like fastball. If he has another go-to pitch, batters will
have to guess what's coming in many situations. Moving the ball around
can also keep a hitter guessing. Therefore, to reduce any great pitcher

down to one pitch, to say, "Oh, sure Johnson is a big winner, he's got that great fastball," is ludicrous. Pitchers know they must develop a pitch to go with their fastball.

Hoffman pointed out, "Your margin for error is definitely greater if you throw harder. The guys [batters] have to make their decisions quicker, they don't have as much time to see the baseball, but strike one is still the best pitch in baseball whether it's at 95 or 85 [mph]."

Another routine "secret" is to change the hitter's eye level. Throwing a low ball to a hitter two times in a row could work and result in a count of, say, 1-1 or 0-2. Fine—now a good idea would be to come up high. The batter will hopefully take it for a high (but with today's umps it can't be too high) strike or swing and miss. When pitchers try to confuse batters by changing their eye level, it's much like yet another ancient tip: "Pitch 'em high and tight, then low and away."

Again, pitchers can deceive batters by mixing up speeds and spots. A hitter can be looking for a given pitch, but the pitcher can still fool him, even when throwing the pitch the batter is sitting on, if he changes speeds and/or location.

Say a hitter has just teed off on a fastball, but got ahead of it and pulled it foul. To throw another pitch of that same speed on the next pitch is ill-advised. Coming back instead with a curve or changeup, while also placing the ball in a different location, is a wiser choice.

Some pitchers even try to fool hitters by occasionally giving them "a different look." That can include dropping the arm down on a delivery now and then, or even lobbing up an odd pitch such as the eephus ("nothing" pitch) or blooper. The blooper pitch was first made famous by Rip Sewell, who would throw a lazy pitch way up in the air, higher than a basketball rim, not unlike a slow-pitch softball delivery. Only once was it launched for a homer. That took place when Ted Williams supplied all the power needed to take it deep in the 1946 All-Star game at Fenway Park, with the game already put away. Even then, Williams, who had just seen one blooper, told Sewell to throw it again. Sewell complied and Williams, aware of what was coming, deposited the blooper into the right-field bullpen.

Many pitchers also believe that they should not throw changeups to weak hitters (especially against young ones). To do so is to do them a favor.

Frank Robinson was the manager of the Expos in 2002, and he took this theory so far as to instruct his pitchers never to throw a straight pitch of any kind to an opposing pitcher.

One technique pitchers often employ is that of making concessions to age. Some older pitchers, hoping to cling to their big-league career as long as they can, will do virtually anything to linger. Spahn, already past the age of retirement for most pitchers, added a screwball to his bag of tricks.

Late in his career, Jim Kaat began quick pitch tactics to keep hitters off stride, as a sort of gimmick pitch. He pitched to the tempo of "Flight of the Bumblebee." Barely, or rarely, letting them get set in the box, he'd get the ball back from the catcher, and, boom, the next pitch was on its way. Only by asking the umpire repeatedly for time out could a batter dig in on Kaat. For that matter, a not-so-old Wakefield, facing the choice of changing positions or quitting the game, made himself into a knuckleball pitcher, adding years and years to an otherwise moribund career.

In 2002 Hoffman, although at 34 hardly a geezer, but not as fast as he had been in his youth, commented on late-career adjustments: "I think that the guys who have the ability to transcend generations or era, have the ability to be a little more fine-tuned with their location. I would hope that my career is nowhere being close to the end, but I've seen a difference in how I used to throw—I was in the mid-90s, and now I'm in, roughly, the mid-80s, upper-80s on some good days. But I still have the ability to be effective by location.

"But I think guys will have success later in their careers if they can apply the experience they've had, the amount of time that they've been on the hill and know that there's as much pressure on the hitter as there is [on] them and to be able to locate a fastball and work off of that."

As for Hoffman messing around with a gimmick pitch such as the knuckler to stick around, he firmly said that was out of the question. "We've seen a lot of knuckleball pitchers, and they're either really on or they're really off," Hoffman said. "And in this role [closer] I don't think there's a place for it."

A rather defensive pitching technique for pitchers is how to combat a batter who tries to look back and see where the catcher is setting up prior to a pitch being delivered. Reliever Scott Stewart speculated on how he would handle that situation: "Yeah, I would probably call the catcher out and tell him he's peeking. If we saw him again, we would probably set up away and throw in.

"I don't know, I mean, there's a lot of peeking going on but there's also *not* a lot of peeking going on—you really have to be sure if you think a guy's [really] looking [to gain an edge]." The mild-mannered Stewart sounded as if the situation where he's positive the batter was "cheating" hasn't come up yet, while at the same time implying he didn't really want to brush back or hit a guy unless he was sure the opponent was trying to get that edge.

The rhythm of pitching, another key component in a hurler's technique, can be as simple as the cadence of a troop of soldiers marching. Mazzone says that on the first beat, or count, the pitcher will take a short stride back while bringing his arms over his head or up to his letters. Then, on the second beat, he is to plant his foot in front of the rubber while hoisting the lead leg "to be squared with the rubber. On the count of three," Mazzone wrote, "you shift your weight forward, break your hands, and bring the pitching arm into its unloading position—the high three-quarter or overhand slot." At the fourth beat the ball is released.

Young starters would be wise to learn another lesson about finding a groove on the mound. Perhaps the most dangerous inning for pitchers, one that they sometimes don't survive, is the first inning. Feeling out of sync, perhaps because they warmed up on the bullpen mound and the actual mound isn't the same, they struggle.

If they make it out of that inning, they'll probably be facing the lower end of the batting order to open the second. One way a pitcher may rediscover his rhythm is by going back to the basics of the pitching game, throwing fastballs. Great pitchers will then recover and perhaps even go on to win a game that began with a first-inning debacle.

Like hitters, sometimes a pitcher finds himself in a groove—his pitches are where he wants them to be and things seem easy, almost automatic. Justin Speier explained, "Mechanics has a lot to do with it. If you have sound mechanics and you're doing the same thing all the time, then, yeah, you're going to get to that point a little quicker." Once there, many pitchers want to work rather fast—get the ball and go, since they're locked in.

One seemingly odd tip for a young pitcher is to develop a good memory for how he got people out after enjoying a fine stint on the mound, but conveniently have a poor memory regarding bad outings. Relievers especially learn they have to put a bad performance behind them and move on, since they may have to take to the mound the very next day.

As far as a starter's viewpoint, Cubs fireballer Kerry Wood commented, "Whatever I do out there, I have to forget. Whether it's good or bad I have to forget it, because I have another start in five days." Clearly, five days is a long time to anguish over a bad showing, so it's best to wipe the slate clean.

Kenny Rogers spoke of the coy game that is the very essence of the pitcher versus hitter war. While it's important to throw strikes, for instance, you can't groove many without having to back up third base or home after surrendering long hits (or, worse, wind up taking a quick shower).

Likewise, in a situation calling for a fastball, a pitcher must remain deceptive. In other words, Rogers said quite simply, "You try not to throw what they're looking for, and if they're looking for it, you try to throw it [to a certain] location. You've just got to know your opposition and what their weaknesses are. But you really have to know yourself and your strengths."

Jim Palmer excelled at deceiving hitters. Sometimes he'd achieve that by shaking off his catcher's signs. Palmer wrote in his book *Pitching*, "Say the catcher calls for a fastball. I'll shake him off, and keep shaking him off until he calls for a fastball again. Constant shaking off of signs is bound to make the hitter edgy."

He felt that ploy was highly effective on a count such as 2-2 when the hitter is drooling, waiting for a fastball. Palmer said, "My shaking my head ruins his train of thought."

Steve Woodard said he feels that many of the mental games played between pitchers and hitters may have died down, but they're still around "a little bit.

"For me," he said, "it's setting a guy up. If you don't throw 100 miles an hour, you've got to set guys up [in order] to get them out—maybe with one pitch, or two pitches to set them up. Maddux is probably one of the best; that's somebody you can always follow and look at. He makes guys look silly."

Maddux, however, doesn't always play Mensa-like games with the hitter. He was quoted in the book *Pitch Like a Pro* as saying when he gets a hitter in an 0-2 hole, his goal is "to take him out immediately. I'm going right after him, no fooling around with wasting a pitch up high or throwing one in the dirt." He feels that it may be traditional to waste a pitch in that situation, but that it's also ludicrous.

He has noticed that when pitchers do waste an 0-2 pitch, the ball is so far out of the strike zone that hitters aren't even tempted to chase it—the pitch truly becomes a waste for the pitcher; it doesn't even set up or help out on the next pitch. "If anything," he stated, "it gives the hitter more of an advantage because he gets to see one more pitch come out of your hand."

The great ones can ignore conventions while those who fear giving up a hit on an 0-2 count don't help themselves—all they do is escape the wrath or second-guessing of their manager and fans. They're locked into old-school thinking that probably should have died out as the game evolved and grew more sophisticated. After all, if a thinking man such as Maddux is convinced the traditional 0-2 logic is faulty, perhaps more pitchers should follow suit. Maddux even contends that there are more wild pitches, passed balls, and hit batsmen on 0-2 than on any other count.

Again from *Pitching*, Palmer instructs young pitchers to consider taking a bigger stride if they find themselves throwing the ball a bit low. Conversely, to combat high throws, a pitcher should probably shorten up.

He said that he "used to draw a line with my heel from the middle of the rubber toward home plate. I made sure that my left foot landed on the left side of the line and, obviously, that my right foot went on the right side of the line." He would check his footprints to see how he was striding and to check if he was landing in the same location each time. He said that was his way of making sure he wasn't throwing across his body.

At times, the Atlanta Braves have their pitchers warm up with a crude baseball batter mannequin standing at the plate to give the pitchers the illusion of a real batter digging in against them. Years ago Palmer said that he felt it helped to have a hitter standing there as he practiced. He liked to see how his curves broke "in respect to the hitter."

Pitching coaches from coast to coast shout out the advice, "Don't fly open." They want their pitcher's front shoulder tucked in. Failure to do this can result in the ball moving in undesirable directions. For example, instead of a pitch hitting the inside corner in a righty-versus-righty scenario, the ball may break back over the heart of the plate. For that matter, a curve may still break for the pitcher, but not sharply—it might simply hang, providing a feast for the hitters.

Truth is, some of the best bits of advice are simple. "Let 'em hit it and let your defense work for you," is another trite but true baseball idiom. There's that bit of Little League advice that states a pitcher should "just throw the ball over the plate, let them hit it, and allow your defense to do the job." Dave Burba actually did just that during his August 20 outing in 2000—and it worked at the big-league level. "After I got that 9–0 lead," he stated, "I threw batting practice. I didn't throw many splits. I didn't throw many curveballs. I threw batting practice."

He admitted he was a bit surprised by his success, saying, "I'm sitting on the bench after I struck out Rickey Henderson on a batting practice fastball, and I wondered, 'Why can't it be like this all the time?' You spend all this time in between starts working on mechanics and your breaking ball, and then you win a game by basically throwing batting practice."

Shortly after Burba's outing, Finley turned in a similar performance. That time his manager, Charlie Manuel, observed, "Chuck Finley did a good job. He threw the ball over the plate and let them hit it. He was not trying for strikeouts. He was letting the fielders do their job."

Finley said of that showing, "I tend to go out and try to work corners, but tonight I wanted to take a little more of the plate and keep the ball down." He threw to the middle of the plate instead of trying to be too cute with his location and it worked. Although he entered that game with an average of 8.1 strikeouts per nine innings of work, that night he struck out only 1 through seven innings (89 pitches). What counted most was that he won the game.

7

Cheating on the Mound

ALTHOUGH IT'S NOT legal, one of baseball's "dirty" secrets of pitching success is cheating. If there's a way to deface a baseball, a pitcher will discover it. They scuff and scar, smear and soil, and otherwise "doctor" the baseball in order to gain any edge they can.

Men such as Gaylord Perry, Whitey Ford, Joe Niekro, Lew Burdette, and Rick Honeycutt have used items ranging from K-Y jelly to sandpaper to a thumbtack sticking through a Band-Aid to weave their illegal magic. In 2003, Montreal's Zach Day put Super Glue on a finger of his pitching hand. Such a practice isn't rare for men of the mound trying to prevent a blister from popping. However, it is considered illegal, and when umpires found the foreign substance, he was ejected.

Actually, in the old days, any pitcher could load up a pitch, throwing a spitball with immunity. The illegality of such pitches wasn't established until 1920, and even then, with a grandfather clause, two pitchers per team could be declared a spitball pitcher and continue to ply their trade. The last of the spitballers was Burleigh Grimes, who quit after the 1934 season.

Over the years, the illegal pitches, now generically called the spitball, have actually had such colorful names as the shine ball and the emery ball. Whether the ball is doctored so it's smoother on one side (as is the case with the shine ball), or whether the ball is scuffed, the result is the same.

Further, in the early days of baseball often only two balls were used throughout the entire game, and a veteran pitcher could use the scuffed, soiled, and/or darkened ball to his advantage.

Many pitchers had their own way of fooling umpires and opponents. Cleveland star Mike Garcia had an unusual way of loading up his spitter. "When I'm going to throw one," he confessed, "just after I release the previous pitch I spit into my glove. Everybody is following the ball and nobody sees me do it."

Perry had several other devious tricks. First, he'd fidget with his uniform, especially touching his cap by his (sparse) hair. Even when he wasn't loading up an illegal pitch, he wanted to make the hitters think he might be doing just that. Planting that idea kept them off stride, much to Perry's perverse pleasure and advantage. Later in his career, he came up with a sort of "poof" pitch, or "puff ball," when he'd put what seemed like a couple of kilos of chalky substance from the rosin bag on his hand. Then, when he'd release the pitch, the ball seemed to emerge out of a cloud of white, which was very deceptive to hitters.

They say Ford could take a ball with a cut on it and make it come to the plate doing everything but whistle "Dixie." Some pitchers would enlist their catchers to mar the ball, often cutting it on the buckles of their shin guards. Another tactic was for a catcher to hold the ball in his bare hand preparatory to lobbing it back to the mound after a pitch. Then, the catcher would pretend to lose his balance a bit. To regain his equilibrium, he'd brace himself by placing his bare hand on the ground. His trick: he'd rest his weight on the ball, still clutched in that hand, which in turn pressed dirt into the seams of the ball on one side. Now, the ball, like a spitter, was slightly off balance—enough to get the next pitch to dip wildly.

When Honeycutt was with Seattle he faced Kansas City, and soon the K.C. hitters suspected foul play as Honeycutt's pitches broke erratically and sank wildly. So, they collected several balls that had been fouled off and discovered they had identical slash marks on them. The umpire examined Honeycutt and spotted a flesh colored bandage on the index finger of his glove hand and, more telling, a thumbtack sticking up through the bandage. Later a piece of sandpaper fell out of his glove indicating that he was both cutting and "bruising" the ball. All that earned him an ejection and a 10-day suspension.

During a 1987 contest Joe Niekro denied he had scuffed baseballs using an emery board (one source said he used sandpaper). He protested his innocence even though umpires found the illegal "device" in his uniform pocket when they strip-searched him, so to speak, on the mound in front of fans and players alike. Being a knuckler, Joe contended that he always had to keep his fingernails filed properly in order to hold his knuckleball just right; he further commented that he therefore had not cheated, nor had any official ever produced evidence of any defacing of the baseballs he had thrown that day.

In August of 2002, as a Texas Ranger, Kenny Rogers came within six outs of throwing his second perfect game. He came up short of perfection, but won a 3–2 contest. During the game he was accused of scuffing the ball during his outing. "There were scuff marks on five or six balls all in the same place," said Milton Bradley of the Indians. "He had a sharp fingernail or something [illegal]."

Videotape clearly showed him digging his thumbnail into or next to the seam of the ball. Rogers simply declared, perhaps evasively, "They're not going to find anything on me. I don't carry anything on me."

While the spitter may be illegal, Burdette, a noted spitball practitioner, said, "They talk as if all you had to do to throw a spitball was to crank up and throw one. Don't they know it's the hardest pitch there is to control? It takes a lot of practice." Plus, a spitter that doesn't bite, doesn't move, is much like a hanging knuckleball, a fat pitch to hit. Because of these negatives, some people have even proposed legalizing the pitch.

When Chicago Cubs slugger Sammy Sosa was caught with a corked bat in 2003, Terry Mulholland said baseball should really get rid of such bats "or bring back the spitball to even the playing field."

Next is the steroid issue. In 2002, Rogers told *Sports Illustrated* that the use of steroids had permeated not only hitters, but pitchers as well.

"Just look around," he was quoted as saying. "You've got guys in their late 30s, almost 40, who are throwing the ball 96 to 99, and they never threw that hard before in their lives. I'm sorry. That's not natural evolution."

In the article a veteran infielder alleged the biggest change he had observed in baseball was the advent of middle relievers who fired the ball at around 92 mph. He said that in the past those pitchers normally topped out in the mid-80s. They quoted the unidentified player as commenting, "Now everybody is throwing gas, including the last guy in the bullpen."

The cat-and-mouse game in baseball doesn't exactly qualify as cheating, but it comes close. Former big-leaguer Scott Pose stated that duplicity still goes on. "Sometimes a guy will 'fan' his glove or nod," Pose said. "Or the 'shake off' is another thing that they try to do to mess with you — they'll do this rub, make you think more [about what pitch he's telling his catcher he wants to throw] than you normally will."

He elucidated on the "fan" move employed by pitchers. "Pitchers, when they get their signs, some guys will fan their gloves out like they're really moving the ball around [to get a certain grip/to throw a certain pitch]. When they get a sign, this [a gesture to the chest area] either means, 'Yeah, I like that pitch, but I want a different location,' or, 'No, it's the next sign [I want].'" He indicated such tactics are ploys to mess with the batter's mind.

"If you see a guy shift around, some guys tip their pitches and give them away," Pose continued. "Then, of course, a pitcher could do that to their advantage where, 'It may look like I'm throwing this, but I'm doing something else.' There are just a lot of nuances going on."

8

Catchers' Influence

THE "INSIDE" GAME of trickery that began over 100 years ago in baseball is still going on. It happens most often between the pitcher (in league with his catcher) and the batter and, more broadly, between the defense and the offense.

Catcher Tom Lampkin has said that if he notices an opposing hitter move in the batter's box "it's a possibility that as a catcher we can try to call different pitches [to cross up the hitter who is obviously looking for a certain pitch]." He added that a catcher must beware that the hitter isn't decoying him, pretending to be sitting on a certain pitch when in reality he's setting the pitcher up, fooling him. It's a case of spy-versus-spy moves and countermoves.

Another indirect way for a pitcher to help himself is to make sure, with the further help of coaches, that his catcher isn't giving his signs away to the opposition. Michael Barrett said, "There are first base coaches in the league that are constantly looking in for the catchers' signs or looking where the catcher is going to set up, relaying the signs to the hitter—or the third base coach [doing this] for left-handed hitters. There are always coaches or players trying to get an edge, an advantage over the other team. You have to be careful."

Most umpires are too savvy to be duped by blatant attempts by a catcher at framing pitches; if a catcher snatches at the ball and jerks it back over the strike zone, he'll be scolded rather than rewarded. However, if a catcher is subtle with the movement of his mitt, he may be able, at times, to steal a strike for his pitcher. Like any skill, some catchers are better than others at framing the ball. Arizona reliever Koplove actually believes an effective catcher can "steal" as many as two pitches per inning.

Yet another way a catcher can help his pitcher is contributing to the meetings on the mound when a pitcher is struggling. Fans often wonder what is being said out there on the hill. Barrett said, "It depends on the pitcher. Every pitcher is different, unique. Some guys you have to motivate and some guys you have to calm down. Some guys you have to encourage, some guys you have to pump up or pump down—it just depends."

Often during a game a catcher will empathize or philosophize with his pitcher. He may egg him on with words of encouragement or try to rile him to action with harsher expressions. If a pitcher, for example, is getting lazy with his pitches, his catcher might fire the ball back to him instead of lobbing it. A field general such as catching great Carlton Fisk was notorious for using such tactics to get his pitcher back on track.

While most big-league hitters are unafraid of being hit by a pitch, Lampkin said, "I know some guys who are [afraid]. And, as a catcher, you can end up getting an advantage by throwing balls inside to [those] people."

Clearly then, a catcher can help his pitcher enjoy more success by being observant. Lampkin added, "Luckily, the more time you spend in the league, the more time you get to know some of these guys and know who the thinkers are and who the guys are who try to [set up the pitchers]."

One way pitchers and catchers learn is, he said, from "guys who move around teams so much who talk about guys that they played with, and you try to remember stuff like that when [those players that you've informally 'scouted'] come up to the plate."

If a pitcher hadn't seen a batter for quite some time—say, from spring training to midsummer—and that hitter had altered his stance and/or positioning in the box, would a pitcher notice it? Scott Stewart said, "Usually I don't catch it; the catcher [sees] all that or maybe the shortstop [might]." So pitchers, standing 60 feet 6 inches away from the plate, often do rely on their catchers to be their eyes.

Their eyes, yes, and even their brains at times. While many pitchers feel the choice of a pitch should be theirs—since ultimately they take responsibility for the results of having thrown a given pitch—young pitchers often rely on their catcher at first. Looking back on his early days when he put total faith in his veteran catchers, Charles Nagy commented, "You learn with experience how to take control of a game. Whatever they put down, I threw, but you learn to trust yourself and your ability. You have to pitch the way you did in the minors, the way that got you here. It comes with confidence; you'll shake the catcher off. You know what you can do [eventually]."

When it came to knowing umpires' strike zones, Lee Smith said, "I really relied on my catcher." Normally he was just shooting for his catcher's target, but he revealed that he had input, having "a sign for my fastball in and one for my fastball away." Thus, if his catcher put down one finger for a fastball, it meant a fast one inside. If Smith shook him off, he wasn't shaking off a fastball, but rather its location. So, when he looked in again, his catcher might well be showing the two-fingers sign, and if Smith agreed with that pitch selection, he would then throw his outside heater, "and all my infielders and outfielders knew the same."

If a pitcher having faith in his catcher's pitch-calling is important, so, too, is his trust in his ability to block pitches in the dirt. That's especially true with so many pitchers today throwing last-second, big breaking pitches and, of course, splitters, which plunge to the dirt quite often (and quite precariously when men are on base).

Pitchers with great gloves working for them behind home plate will throw, for example, the splitter with no reservations, but a pitcher with a shaky defensive catcher might have to shelve his valuable splitter in crucial moments—just the time he really wants to use that pitch. So, again, there is no doubt that one secret of good pitching is actually having good catching.

One source said that Koufax started to become a great pitcher when Joe Becker, a former catcher, worked with the great lefty and tinkered with his delivery until finally Koufax became comfortable with his stuff.

Good catchers are students of the game, with many going on to base-ball's managerial ranks. Lately, they own a monopoly on World Series rings. Joe Torre, a former catcher and veteran of eight All-Star contests, guided his Yankees to championship titles in 1996, 1998, 1999, and 2000, incredibly winning it all in four of his first five years in New York. Then two more ex-catchers won the Series crown in 2001 and 2002: Bob Brenly and Mike Scioscia, respectively.

Smith dished out more praise for receivers, saying that having a good catcher "means so much. I liked the big, wide-bodied guy so that you can throw that ball about four inches off the plate and the umpire couldn't tell if it was a strike or not. Jody Davis and Rich Gedman were beautiful guys; Jody was about 6'4", about 230, and you got the borderline pitches. If you threw that ball down there and it looked like a strike, good height and it looked like it was right off the plate, you got the borderline pitch and that's when you get the hitter to start swinging at the borderline pitches."

Smith said umps don't mind the pitcher or catcher "asking about a pitch, but they don't like you to ask during the heat of the battle. I asked while I was walking off the field in between innings. They don't want to be shown up, so I didn't ask during an at-bat. I had enough respect for the man to ask him when the inning was over."

On one occasion when Smith was young, he questioned a ball call by the ump, which favored a veteran hitter. The umpire rebuffed Smith who later said, "Needless to say, I didn't ask him again." Lesson learned.

When Carl Erskine threw his second no-hitter, he said he did it with "a good fastball and my control was all right. I used more changeup pitches than the first time." Then he credited his catcher, Roy Campanella. "Campy was wonderful. He kept slowing me down. I never saw him so deliberate."

Catchers do feel a responsibility for their pitchers. In 2002, Gregg Zaun was the personal catcher for Dave Mlicki. Frustrated after a loss, Zaun said, "I've got to figure out a way to get him going."

In return, pitchers can develop a fierce loyalty for their catchers. For instance, Greg Maddux has had his own personal "caddy" for years, at times being linked with Eddie Perez, Damon Berryhill, and, more recently, with Henry Blanco.

While it's true that pitchers who throw in the dirt a lot (e.g., split-finger artists) rely upon the kindness and dexterity of catchers, submarine pitcher Kent Tekulve, interestingly enough, said the catcher's role when he threw was diminished. One of his catchers, Manny Sanguillen, had the uncanny ability to hunker lower to the ground than a limbo dancer, yet Teke said that prowess wasn't crucial to his game.

"Not really. I mean, I don't think it was as important for us [submariners] as it was for the power pitchers because our idea was we wanted the guy to hit the ball. We didn't want him to swing and miss. The catcher was more back there for a target, something to aim at, to throw at, but you wanted the guy to hit it. So, actually the successful pitches were the ones that never got to the catcher anyway—those were the ground balls in the infield."

9

The Bullpen

Tom Henke, an outstanding reliever, had a theory about closing pitchers. "You only need to master two pitches as a closer, but it never hurts to have an extra pitch." With that in mind, he fooled around with a forkball, using it for an off-speed pitch.

Henke was typical of most bullpen inhabitants, who often toy around with their stuff. They talk a lot of baseball to while away the long hours in the pen, and they experiment with various grips and deliveries to improve their game.

Lee Smith spoke of another key to being the main man of the bullpen. "You can't be intimidated, especially if you're going to be considered the closer." He said he never had the feeling that there was a batter that he couldn't retire. Additionally, he said that if you let a hitter get to you, say, after hitting a tape-measure home run, then you are in trouble.

"If you do that," he critiqued, "then he's gonna hit one a little farther the next time. But guys like that who hit long home runs have a lot of holes you can pitch to. Sometimes you make a mistake and don't get it there and you get hurt bad, but there's not one guy [I fear].

"There hasn't been a .400 hitter in a long time, and even then the man made 6 outs out of every 10. You gotta take your chances just like everybody else."

Smith, well aware of the importance of experience for relievers, said he could understand some pitchers being intimidated. "I can see rookies would be [afraid]. You take a young guy and send him in there to Detroit [of their Kirk Gibson et al. era] in his first game and he gives up 12 runs.

"Then the next time, probably against the Tigers again, and he's gonna remember! After a while—if you're going to be around a while—you've got to really adjust to hitters."

When Jose Mesa was lights-out with the Indians in the mid-1990s, his pitching coach, Mark Wiley, stated, "All the good closers are strike-throwers. [With Mesa] the hitters knew they had to swing or they'd be down 0-1. He made them commit."

Meanwhile, Danys Baez of the Cleveland Indians has spent time in both the bullpen and the starting rotation. He spoke of how he had to learn to prepare to take to the mound under diverse circumstances. First, out of the pen: "You throw fastball, curveball, splitter, whatever. You have to know what kind of pitches you have to throw at a [certain] time, but you have a routine and everybody's [routine] is different.

"When you're in the starting rotation, you have more time. You have five days to work out and do your running and before the game you have more time to throw. But in the bullpen, when the telephone rings, you have to go and throw and get ready in 15, 20 pitches."

Another big difference experienced by men who have started and relieved is the novelty factor. That is, if a pitcher has one pitch that he throws a huge percentage of the time, he has a much better chance of getting away with that, of fooling hitters, if he works out of the bullpen. The reason? A batter may only see a reliever for one at-bat in a game or perhaps even for an entire series. With a starter, he'd get several chances to see that out pitch, acclimate himself to it, and eventually solve the pitch.

The bullpen is all about warming up. In May of 1999, Cleveland bullpen coach Luis Isaac said, "I catch all the starting pitchers on the day they warm up. Starting pitchers usually throw between 60 and 90 pitches when they are warming up." However, he, too, stated, "Each pitcher has a different routine." For the record, the least amount of warm-up pitches needed by an Indians starter that year was around 68, by Jaret Wright. The most was Burba's 85 or so.

"Relievers are different," Isaac continued. "They usually have to be able to get ready in about 20 warm-up pitches. If they are not in the game after that, I'll tell them to slow down and watch the game a little between throws. You don't want them throwing so many pitches in the bullpen that they don't have anything left when they get into the game."

Clearly, each pitcher requires a certain amount of preparatory work, and it varies quite a bit from one man to another. Billy Wagner once took 50–70 pitches but said that now, as a veteran reliever, he is ready to go in 15–20 tosses. Steve Karsay said he has got it down to 12–15 pitches, 20 at the max, to get his arm nice and loose.

Hoffman is an extreme case, a man who strives never to wear his arm out by expending a lot on warm-up throws. He's been known to enter a game after making only one toss from the bullpen mound. Instead of using the traditional approach, he makes throws from in front of and even from behind the mound to stretch his arm out.

He told *USA Today/Baseball Weekly,* "I know when I get to the pitching mound I have eight throws to get ready. When I'm in the bullpen, I try to judge how many throws I'll need to take so that I'll be ready on my eighth warm-up toss from the regular mound."

Wiley kept track of how many times one of his pitchers warmed up during the game. He did this to prevent a reliever from burning himself out while still in the bullpen, a very real risk.

Karsay said he feels he's been asked to warm up too many times when he's been called upon to get up and throw "three or more [times]. Three's a lot to get warm — in three different innings of the ball game, and then maybe get into the game and pitch a couple of innings. Two, and then go in the game [is OK], but once you get up to a third time, I think it takes the wind out of your sails." If he has to get up three times, he typically expends around 45–60 tiring pitches. "Then you got to make some pitches in the ball game." It all adds up.

Karsay insisted that managers try to avoid overthrowing by the bullpen, but admitted, "There are situations where you can't, like when you're in a pennant race, but the later you pitch in a ball game, the less of a chance you have for that to happen. It happens more with a long reliever in case the starter gets into trouble a few times."

Because relievers throw irregular "hours," their rest schedule is also different than starters who know when their off days will fall. Relievers get their off days any chance the manager has to give them a blow—say, during a laugher.

Bruce Sutter summed up what, for him, was the ideal workload out of the bullpen: "I [wouldn't] pitch a lot of games in a row and I [wouldn't] go a long time without pitching." In other words, he'd stay sharp and never be forced into a situation where he'd get rusty, either. Relievers such as Mike Marshall, who wanted the ball virtually each day, are the exceptions. He once worked 13 games in a row, and established another all-time high when he threw in an astronomical 106 games over 208 mind- (and arm-) numbing innings in 1974.

While it may seem odd, a pitcher or a pitching coach cannot judge, based on how a starting pitcher warms up in the bullpen prior to the game, if that starter has good stuff *and* will be effective in the game that day. Sometimes a starter will feel he has great stuff and it does carry over to the game, but sometimes the opposite holds true.

On August 8, 1991, Charles Nagy had what his bullpen catcher that night called "very close to Charlie's worst stuff of the year." Pitching Coach Rick Adair agreed. "We're in deep trouble," he predicted. "Charlie's got nothing." Nagy, who admitted he couldn't throw a strike while warming up, then came within a scratch infield hit of throwing a no-hitter.

One secret of getting ready in the bullpen is to understand one's role. If a pitcher can do that, he can often anticipate, based on game conditions, when the call will come to the bullpen. "If you're a set-up man or closer, you know what kind of situation it is—if they're going to call you or not," concluded Baez.

Some pitchers like to have a man stand near the plate when they warm up. Some feel it helps them prepare for what they'll really face in the game, while others feel it allows them to picture a strike zone.

Meanwhile, Hoffman told *Sports Illustrated* that he has a pattern he follows during each game to "remove [him] from the intensity of the situation." He begins by observing the first five innings of games from the bullpen. Then he banishes himself to the clubhouse, where he loosens up by taking a hot shower (making him a rare pitcher to hit the showers before being forced to do so) and by stretching. By the time he returns to the pen, it's usually pretty close to the time he begins to warm up prior to a ninth-inning entrance, accompanied by his theme song, "Hell's Bells" by AC/DC.

Relievers seldom speak of pain to the public, but Cleveland's Scott Stewart candidly said that when it comes to the amount of rest it takes for the pain to abate after a day on the mound, "It never goes away. As a reliever it never goes away—once you start hurting, usually you're hurting [the rest of the year]. But it's not really a hurt, it's just an aching because you're throwing so much."

There are stories of pitchers whose arms hurt so much after a performance they couldn't raise them, not even to do a simple chore like brushing their hair. Stewart said he's had days where his arm was really "sore, but not really *that* bad. I don't throw hard enough to have that [occur]."

Smith said that when the 300-save club numbered five, they were all gathered in Florida one day and "all they talked about was being consistent. And when the manager calls on you, say that you're ready. He didn't have to call and check, 'Well, can you throw today?' The answer was always yes.

"Joe Torre was one of my favorite managers. He'd just say, 'Hey, Smitty, you need a day off?' I'm like, 'Yeah, I'll take one off in November. I'm playing the game, man, I'm ready to play. That's why I come here for; I don't come here to watch the game—I could sit in the bleachers to do that.' I liked to throw a lot."

Smith had only six starts during his great career. His move to the pen came, he said, "when they found out that I could throw four, five days in a row. You find a lot of pitchers who [like me] didn't have a defined position—I came up as a starter and they [the Cubs] had guys like Fergie Jenkins, Mike Krukow, and Rick Reuschel. And in the bullpen, as a closer, they had Bruce Sutter.

"I spot started a couple of times, but more than that I was a middle reliever and set-up man. Then when they found out that day after day I got stronger [things changed]. 'We got a good relief pitcher here, a guy who likes to throw every day.' You don't find too many guys, power pitchers, who are able to throw three or four days in a row."

Interestingly, Smith was not glad to make the move to become a bullpen dweller. "As a matter of fact," he stated, "when I was first made a relief pitcher in Triple-A, I quit playing baseball and went back to Northwestern [in Louisiana] and played college basketball. At the time, it was a slap in the face to be a reliever. It was like, 'Oh, the guy's not good enough to be a starter.' They tossed him in the bullpen and tried to hide him, but the role has really defined itself now."

As for today's trend toward bullpen specialization, Smith reflected on how the roles of the bullpen have evolved. He recalled the time when men such as Ron Davis, who was skilled enough to be a closer—in fact, good enough to shut the door when he became a member of the Twins— was used by the Yankees in a set-up role for Goose Gossage. People began seeing the set-up man as being not merely a stopgap measure, but a key ingredient in the pen. Now, the "hold" is an important statistic, and men such as Davis led the way here. Seeing a lefty enter the game to get one out was once unheard of, but is now a matter of routine.

"When I was with St. Louis," began Smith, "we had about three relievers who had more appearances than innings pitched—a Ricky Horton would come in to get Darryl Strawberry, and that was it. The guys knew what their role was. One year he had 22 innings pitched, or something like that, but he came in as a left-handed specialist and Tony Fossas did the same thing. He came into the big leagues as a specialist, to come in and get that one tough lefty and then he's out of the game."

Smith attributes the evolution to the fact that "a lot of managers like [playing] percentages: left-handed pitcher against left-handed hitter. More often than not, left-handed hitters don't hit left-handed pitchers well. There are very few lefties that bear down really hard against left-handed pitching."

So, as for the defined roles of relievers, Smith said, "I think it makes it a lot easier when guys can come and prepare themselves [for their specific job]. There aren't very many teams that have done that bullpen-by-committee thing, over a period of years, that they're trying in Boston. That's not going to work. [It was scrapped after only three months in 2002.] You've got five guys that could come in one day and close, and then [another day one of them] is called in the fourth inning and he's like, 'Well, man, I wasn't ready because I thought I was going to pitch in the seventh inning on.' That's an excuse he can use.

"When you come to that ballpark you [should] know what your job is: if I'm going to pitch the eighth or ninth inning, I prepare myself to pitch the eighth or ninth inning. It's the same thing with a left-handed specialist and a set-up man."

In a way, he expounded, it may not be so much of an excuse as a truth. The pitcher, feeling he might be called upon to close out a game, is out of kilter when he is suddenly thrown into a game in, say, the fourth inning. It's a matter of mind-set for many pitchers.

"I think specialization is smart, but it didn't bother me. As a matter of fact, I think my percentage against left-handed hitters was better than right-handed because I'd probably face five-to-one, lefties to righties, because they'd put them in there against me. It really played to my advantage because I threw the forkball."

He did comment, though, that one factor that hurt some closers occurred "right when they started this only [working the] ninth inning thing, some guys would come in and they pitched an out or two in the eighth inning and they were like, 'I couldn't get my mind-set to go back in in the ninth inning.'

"I didn't do that, I'd pitch when a hitter was out there. I don't care if it was the fifth inning, I took a hitter at a time; I didn't look at the scoreboard and stuff like that, other than, 'OK, I'm in the fifth inning,' I just went out there to pitch.

"When I started closing with Chicago, I was a left-handed specialist, my own set-up man, and, you know, when Rollie Fingers and those guys pitched, they went three innings [unlike today]. As a former starting pitcher, it took me a while as a closer to get that mind-set, away from starting, because I like to throw a lot. I'd go out and throw two innings on days where there wasn't a save opportunity. Now the closer would be bent out of shape [if asked to do that].

"If there's a prime example, [it would be] that one year, you remember, when Bobby Thigpen got the [single season record] 57 saves. Well, I had 31 saves that very same year [1990], and I had about 22 more innings pitched than him—in the National League. In the American League it's tougher because the guys have to be in a jam, more than not, for the closer to come in the game. In the National League, you get pinch hit for and [there's] the flip-flop in situations. It's a lot easier for a manager to make that move to put his closer in the game other than just, 'We got the lead in the eighth inning or the ninth inning—boom, we got to put the closer in the game.'"

A scenario that may well occur nowadays is much like what Smith described, with a starter going seven or eight innings and having expended perhaps only 100 pitches or so. The pitcher says he still feels strong, but some managers will automatically go to the pen, without giving his starter the opportunity to enter the ninth. Smith commented, "It depends on the pitcher and what hitters are coming up. If I've got a Billy Wagner and, say, my starting pitcher went seven, eight innings three or four starts in a row, I figure I can give him a blow because we've got a day off coming.

"A lot of people see that situation and they don't think about [everything]. They say, 'Why'd they take him out? He only had one inning left.' The thing is, they're thinking about September." Smith said it can become a bad situation if the pitcher has to toil too much rather than take the rest. Smith said the pitcher might well go out there and work the ninth inning, but he "actually has to throw 25 pitches to get out of that inning."

He looked at the situation another way. "I think it's really positive thinking for that [starting] pitcher. If that guy goes out there and has a 3–1 lead, and he has them tie the game up in the ninth, he'll be like, 'Well, man, I felt my closer was going to be in there.' He'd already think, 'OK, I did my job.' But you find the great starters, they want to go nine. Roger Clemens doesn't want to come out of the game. Guys like that and Nolan Ryan, but you don't find that in very many guys. [For] some guys now, six innings is a quality start."

Smith made it clear that the great starters feel as if they earned the shot at the ninth, and if anyone was going to lose their game, it would be them and not a reliever. He also indicated there are other factors the average fan never considers. He said he could see the normal starter being given the chance to finish the game off "early in the season—I can understand that, because guys try to build up arm strength, things like that. But when you get into July, August, managers are thinking, 'I don't want to extend him too far and get him into a [bad] situation.' Especially with the young pitchers now, you want to keep them in a positive frame of mind."

Some managers feel that if they're paying closers big bucks, then they need to use them to nail down wins. "Why am I going to pay Robb Nen $12 million and let him sit in the pen? I understand that situation," Smith laughed, "but, later on in the year I like to see my set-up man go the eighth and ninth inning.

"I'll tell you what, my last five or six years closing, I had some pretty good set-up men," said Smith. "I had Todd Worrell, Troy Percival, Ugueth Urbina, Armando Benitez, guys like that. You want to give them something to feel positive about. You know, keep everybody in a good frame of mind.

"Now that they came in with the hold, that helps a lot for negotiating purposes with set-up men who have it tougher than the closers. I would not want to be a set-up man because most of them come in with guys on second and third; closers, most of them, start the ninth inning with the bases empty."

Sometimes yet another way of thinking pops into managers' heads concerning the late-inning use of starters and relievers. Said Smith, they might feel, "If the guy is going to be my ace, he's going to have to show me he's going to be my ace. I'm not going to give it to him."

Smith refuted another theory held by some that teams would be better off giving the ball to a young hard thrower, say just up from the minors, allowing him to be a closer rather than pay out a veritable ransom to the recycled, established relievers. The argument states that all closers, even untested ones, are going to rack up the easy saves while even a veteran closer will blow his share of them.

Smith scoffed, "You know the minor league saves don't matter when you go to the big leagues. It's a different thing out there. You know what, I remember when I'd blow a save and some guys would say, 'Man, what happened?' I'd say, 'Hey, that guy that I was pitching against is a pretty good hitter.'

"They look at closers like they're supposed to do that job [routinely]. When something happens like I make a good pitch and they hit the ball, that's why they call it baseball. But one thing with young guys, they see the numbers on the hitters and they give them too much credit. I say, respect the hitter, but don't give him too much credit and underestimate your ability."

10

The Art of Intimidation

To LISTEN TO baseball "war" stories, especially of grizzled men from "the good ol' days," is to be regaled by tales of legendary pitchers who made batters shake in their spikes. Consider the case of 6'6" Pirates pitcher Bob Veale. He faced Lou Brock one steamy night in the 1960s. At one point Veale called time out to wipe off his glasses, which had fogged up. He was unsuccessful in cleaning them off, so he placed his glasses in his pocket and toed the rubber ready for his next pitch.

In his best imitation of Scooby Doo spotting a ghost, Brock vaulted out of the box. There was no way, Brock informed the ump, that he'd face a Veale fastball when the southpaw had no glasses and consequently no sense of direction. It was bad enough to face big Bob Veale when he *could* see, reasoned Brock.

Early Wynn, a 300-game winner who pitched until he was 43 years old, is still considered to be one of the fiercest pitchers ever. He would drill hitters with a blazing fastball, a pitch that had all the subtlety of bear-baiting, or brush them back with some "chin music," a fastball that buzzed batters near the neck. "I don't like losing a ball game any more than a salesman likes losing a sale," Wynn snarled. "I've got a right to knock down anybody holding a bat." He also summed up his attitude on the mound when he stated, "A pitcher will never be a big winner until he hates hitters."

One Wynn story has it that after Detroit's George Kell singled through the box off the crusty veteran, the pitcher was going to throw over to first base, not to keep Kell close to the bag, but to hit him—to pay him back without having to wait for Kell's next at-bat in order to plunk him!

Another time, according to *Baseball Digest* writer John Steadman, pitcher Tommy Byrne threw at Ted Williams before he even entered the batter's box. Williams and teammate Mickey Vernon were standing about 10 feet from the on-deck circle, near home plate, watching Byrne warm up.

Byrne was quoted as saying, "They weren't timing me, but I think they were trying to catch the velocity on the ball or what kind of movement it had when I was taking my warm-ups." It was then that Byrne fired a ball between the hitters to get them to move back. Imagine, a brushback pitch to a hitter who wasn't even at the plate.

Wynn is followed closely in ferocity by Dodger Don Drysdale. St. Louis infielder Mike Shannon once said that Drysdale "would consider an intentional walk a waste of three pitches. If he wants to put you on base, he can hit you with one."

Clearly, Drysdale, a seven-time All-Star, was a very intimidating player, unafraid to throw more than one pitch in tight to any given batter. "The second one makes the hitter know you meant the first one," said the feisty Drysdale.

Colorful Dizzy Dean would clown around, but on the mound he was as serious as a biopsy. Once, when a hitter was digging in on Dean in the batter's box, he bellowed, "You comfortable? Well, send for a groundskeeper and get a shovel, 'cause that's where they're going to bury you."

Mark Grace related to that tale, saying, "Intimidation works for pitchers—that's what 'chin music' is all about. If a Nolan Ryan or Dwight Gooden throws tight, it sends a message: don't dig in."

Ryan perfected such fear-instilling tactics so well, one player joked, "He's baseball's exorcist; he scares the devil out of you." Reggie Jackson concurred, "Ryan's the only guy who put fear in me, . . . because he could kill me." He said a good game against Ryan was a walk drawn with an otherwise quiet o for 3. Oscar Gamble disagreed, though, saying a good night was "o for 4 and don't get hit in the head."

The very legend of Ryan helped increase the fear factor. As Ken Griffeys Jr. observed, "He's the only one that I felt was different because of stories my dad and Andre Dawson and Shawon Dunston told me . . . that he was mean and nasty."

Going back one baseball generation from Ryan, Sandy Koufax went as far as to define pitching as "the art of instilling fear by making a man flinch."

In order to gain the intimidation imprimatur, outfielder Jay Buhner said a pitcher needed three elements: speed, physical appearance, and sometimes psychology. "When I first came up, Roger Clemens was very intimidating," said Buhner. "Just by the way they carry themselves, guys like Ryan and Goose Gossage were very intimidating people.

"I think more of your intimidating pitchers were your guys who threw harder, but there were still some guys out there that aren't the hardest throwers in the world, but still got in your head. They were smart pitchers like Frank Tanana.

"To me, though, it was more so the big guys who threw hard and gave you 'the look.' And the way they carried themselves, and maybe it's facial hair—the goatee or mustache. The way they pull the hat down over their eyes like Goose [did].

"I mean it's a lot of things—the way they throw their first pitch, or like Nolan Ryan used to come up and stare you down. Everybody's got their own little style."

Gossage certainly did have his own style, even if he didn't try to develop it. "Nothing I did out there was premeditated, that's just the way I am out there," Gossage said. "I never consciously thought about intimidation." He once admitted that his own wife wouldn't know him when he was pitching. He noted, "Hate is an ugly word, but I hate hitters."

Gossage continued: "I never faced a hitter that intimidated me, that I was afraid of. Never." He then added that there was one time when he should have been. "One day I threw one up and in on Willie Horton and it just got away from me when I was a young kid back with the White Sox. He stood there and I got the ball back from the catcher and I walked around the mound. Then I felt something staring right through me; I looked back at home plate and his eyes were as big as saucers. I turned around and went, 'Whoa! This guy can scare you.'

"Then I turned [toward Horton] and said, 'Fuck him, I'm not gonna let him intimidate me,' and I threw another one up and in. It was stupidity, really."

One could argue Gossage was not stupid, but had sent a message and firmly established that he was in the bigs to stay. Pitchers who have had a hard time recovering from such a strong case of "evil eye" intimidation may not make it in the majors. In other words, pitchers must feel they are the intimidator, not the recipient of fear.

As for facial hair, some fans (and players) felt Gossage's mustache helped his tough guy image. Griffey Jr. said he was intimidated by Gossage even when Junior was a young kid. The reason? "That mustache. The way he pulled his hat down over his eyes. He never smiled."

Meanwhile, Smith summed up Gossage's air of confidence and his fear-inducing ways, saying, "I think his 95-mile-an-hour fastball was confidence enough."

Longtime observers of the game recalled how a Gossage prototype employed a beard as a dramatic device. Burleigh Grimes used his stubbly five-o'clock shadow to cause trepidation. He'd never shave prior to a game and his scruffy appearance was imposing. That look also led to his getting the nickname "Ol' Stubblebeard" en route to his 270 lifetime victories.

Interestingly, Gossage downplayed hair as a weapon. "I had success before I had my mustache. It was never an act for intimidation." He said he first grew his 'stache simply to irritate and break the rules of George Steinbrenner, the owner of the Yankees when Gossage was with them.

He also believed Randy Johnson's wild, long hair (at one time) and mustache weren't the key to his success. "I think he's very intimidating, although I don't think he really tries to be. I think that's just the way he carries himself out there—that and throwing hard," he added as an understatement.

Buhner, who faced Johnson in the minors when his control was extremely wild, said, "Let me put it this way, you didn't want to dig in on him."

Meanwhile, Al Hrabosky, with his Fu Manchu, had a countenance that embodied the old line "If looks could kill." Once his manager told him he'd have to shave off his facial growth. Hrabosky snorted, "How can I intimidate batters if I look like a fucking golf pro?" To him, shaving was tantamount to allowing Delilah to do her strength-sapping barber act.

Gossage also had a take on the mound antics of Hrabosky preparatory to pitching. He felt that the "Mad Hungarian" wasn't, or shouldn't have been, all that intimidating. "I think definitely it was an act." Smith believed "he was psyching himself out; I don't think he intimidated anybody. They're big-league hitters, you can't do that to major league hitters—maybe to a young kid that's just coming up, but not anybody who has some time in the big leagues. I don't think you could." Either way, he did get to some opposing batters, often upsetting their timing by taking his strolls behind the mound as he worked himself into a frenzy.

Brad "The Animal" Lesley also went into a wild man act on the mound, not unlike a maniacal version of the *Saturday Night Live* skit involving weight lifters who "want to pump you up." However, former manager Jim Lefebvre felt Lesley's flexing and posturing boomeranged on him. "It cost him his job," Lefebvre said. "There are guys who have very unusual mannerisms, but when you start doing it as a circus act, it backfires. He used to come off the mound and go, 'Raar-hh,' He tried to show you up. My feeling is it was all an act.

"[Eventually] hitters just said, 'This guy's not going to get me out.'" In Lesley's case the intimidation factor waned quickly—he lasted in the majors for only 54 appearances.

Like Wynn, Stan Williams had a hard reputation. He was said to have kept pictures of good hitters such as Frank Robinson inside his locker—to throw at. If he'd do that in the clubhouse, imagine what he'd do on the field. It's not unlike an old line from Whit Wyatt: "You ought to play it mean—they ought to hate you on the field."

Then there was Sal "The Barber" Maglie, who went so far as to say, of his own teammates, "I don't want to get to know the other guys too well—I might like them, and then I might not want to throw at them [if they get traded]." At times, when the count ran to 3-0, he would hit the batter on purpose. His logic was that since the hitter was probably going to draw a walk or get a good pitch to hit, why not put him on anyway while sending a painful message at the same time.

Maglie was despised for years by Dodger fans. Then a trade put him in the Brooklyn flannels. Carl Erskine of the Dodgers said that the players actually had "a respect for him. He'd throw a low number of pitches, 85 or so. He was crafty, he had a hard, extremely sharp curve. He was not a malicious person. His brushback was used to enhance the curve." Even if he wasn't malicious, it's clear he wanted people to think of him as possessing a near-murderous personality.

In the meantime, when Dick "The Monster" Radatz, who stood 6'6", was with the Expos, he once was in the middle of a melee after throwing a brushback pitch. As the brawl warmed up, Radatz encountered the 5'6" Freddie Patek. "Looking at the diminutive infielder with disdain, Radatz muttered, "I'll take you and a player to be named later."

Another man as wild as they come was Ryne Duren. His method of causing fear was to purposely throw erratic warm-up tosses before the start of an inning. And, boy, were his tosses way off the mark, at times hitting off the backstop or netting behind the plate.

Smith had a rather unusual theory about pitching. He said in many situations he "would much rather face a home run hitter with his big swing than to face some of the smaller guys who hit the ball where it's pitched and put the bat on the ball."

Two-time All-Star Gregg Jefferies also had a view concerning the pitcher-hitter battle. "Actually, I don't think pitchers get intimidated, they just have to buckle down more on certain guys." He called it more a matter of respect than fear.

Red Schoendienst seems to agree, saying one can cause fear or respect in pitchers just by being "a good line drive hitter—hit for extra bases like Tony Gwynn. Hitters like that hurt you [deep] once in a while if you make a mistake, but they're not gonna try like the home run hitter. They stay within themselves. That's why they hit for average."

Meanwhile, Mike Hargrove conceded that long, majestic home runs are impressive "because not many people can do it. But I don't think you can intimidate a pitcher [with homers]. The old saying goes, 'No matter how far you hit it, you still get only one run.'"

Then, jokingly, he recalled an Albert Belle shot and said, "Though where he hit it, you ought to get more than one run for hitting a ball that far. But as far as intimidating, no, it's not intimidating [to go deep]. It really is more amazing than anything else."

Perhaps, says Smith, intimidation doesn't exist against hitters, either. He said that factor—such as displaying an arrogant attitude and exuding confidence out of the bullpen—doesn't work on hitters. "No, there aren't any guys in the major leagues that think you can intimidate them. And if they do, they ain't going to be in the big leagues long."

Maybe it's a matter of semantics, as Shuey said, that while hitters don't like pitchers throwing way in on them, to a certain extent batters respect pitchers who aren't afraid to do this, albeit with some limitations. "A guy can gain some respect by showing that he does throw inside occasionally, but it's a different thing when you're throwing at heads.

"You can get the same effect by throwing at somebody's knees, getting them to jump out of the way where they've got a shot at getting out of the way. When you throw at somebody's head, you could really kill somebody. That's not really what you want to do. It's going to happen; I mean, I'll throw at somebody once in a while by accident, but when you're doing it intentionally, and for a purpose, for me it's better to just go hard in by the hip area."

Gerald Williams led off a game during the 2000 season and was hit by a 1-2 pitch from Pedro Martinez. Williams went ballistic. An announcer wondered why he reacted so vehemently. Surely Martinez didn't want the game's first batter getting a free ride to first, especially when the hitter had already been behind in the count?

Shuey said the hitters know "Pedro's been very consistent about smoking people with regularity and usually smoking them right around the face. That's happened to us [the Indians], and that's why we've gotten in brawls with him in the past. Then he usually runs and hides in the dugout—and that's not a good deal there.

"He's maybe the best pitcher in the game right now, [and pitching like] that may be a way to keep guys off edge, and you can do it, but it's certainly not going to make you any friends on the other teams," he stated.

On July 7, 2003, Martinez came in so hard, high, and tight to Alfonso Soriano and Derek Jeter, he hit both on their hand, forcing both to leave the game to get x-rays. Martinez responded to reporters' questions, contending he wasn't trying to hit Soriano. "Are you crazy? The guy's right on top of the plate. The only way you're going to get Soriano out is inside. He hits curveballs, he hits changeups, he leans over the plate. He's that good. You've got to give him a lot of credit. When you throw inside, you're going to hit guys sometimes. I don't try to hit anybody, it was just an accident."

Shuey added that getting brushed back leads to hitters either becoming afraid or angry, and since guys don't last in the majors if they play with fear, their anger will lead to continuing instances of batters charging the mound. Since they're willing to accept fines and suspensions to show they have no fear, fights and intimidation are here to stay.

By August of 2002, Cleveland's Ricardo Rodriguez had gained a reputation of throwing inside, à la a young Martinez. He said, "If I don't pitch inside, I can't pitch. When I was in the minor leagues, I could throw a two-seamer over the plate and usually they wouldn't hit it. Up here, I can't do that. In the big leagues, if I pitch inside and miss, I prefer that the ball go way in. I don't want to hit the guy, but it's better I hit him than the ball goes over the middle of the plate."

In his first major league win, he was ejected for hitting a batter moments after giving up a home run. He said he had no plans to quit throwing tight, because his "family lives there and I live there, too."

Phenom Bob Feller pitched tight from the very first game he ever played in the majors, just off his high school campus. He recalled, "The first strikeout I ever got was in July of 1936 in Washington. In my first inning [in relief of Johnny Allen] I know my first strikeout was of Buddy Lewis. I had thrown too close to the first man I faced, and then came Lewis, and he was nowhere *near* the plate. He *couldn't* have hit the ball; he struck out."

Early on during his career, Bartolo Colon seemed to be the opposite of Feller, avoiding retaliation pitches. When he finally unleashed a wicked knockdown pitch against the A's shortly after his Indians played a few games featuring bad blood between them, his catcher, Sandy Alomar Jr., said, "Bartolo is growing up. This is a big step for him. That's how you earn respect."

Cleveland Plain Dealer writer Paul Hoynes pointed out a huge contrast between the Colon of the evening of his payback and the Colon of just a few years earlier. "Roger Clemens hit Robbie Alomar in a game [in 1999]," wrote Hoynes. "Word was given to Colon to retaliate against Derek Jeter, the leadoff hitter the next inning. Jeter homered off him instead. What's more, he hit the homer to right field, which meant the pitch was away from Jeter.

"That did not go over well in the clubhouse. This time [versus the A's] Colon left no doubt about his intentions," observed Hoynes.

He then quoted Shuey as saying, "Bartolo let him know, 'Yeah, I can kill you just like that.' Guys had been telling him he had to throw inside. I think that's big for us. Maybe it will get him over the hump. I mean you throw 100 *mph*, you should go inside."

In another Cleveland-Oakland fracas, Steve Reed drilled outfielder Eric Byrnes with a pitch. Reed was later asked if he did so intentionally. "Why would I hit him on purpose when I've got him 1-2? On the kid's first swing, he almost did a 360 [degree spin] because he dove out over the plate so far. I can't let him do that, so I tried to come inside with a hard sinker.

"I know they thought I hit him on purpose. I could hear their pitching coach chirping from the dugout. When I stared into the dugout, I didn't hear anything. Then, when I turned my back, I heard him start chirping again. They can say what they want. I'm right here. I'm not that far away," he challenged.

In the newspaper the next day, Hoynes gave another account of what took place. He wrote: "There are player-only rules in baseball. Rookies must learn them or get used for target practice. Oakland's Eric Byrnes made his big-league debut Tuesday at Jacobs Field. On every swing he grunted."

Eric's father, Jim, chuckled, "He'd been hit before, whether it was with a baseball or martial arts. To me it was a compliment that they hit him, because he was swinging hard. That's what he *does*. He plays baseball with a football mentality." He joked that his son saw being hit by a pitch merely "as another way to get on base; he didn't care."

In fact, Eric had such a fine performance that night he was selected as the Player of the Game by the media. However, since he was a rookie, the Indians resented his gung-ho approach.

"You'd think this guy had been in the big leagues for 15 years," said one Tribe veteran. So, in many ways, the fracas was a matter of respect. Lesson learned? Grunt quietly.

11

Intangibles and Other Insights

RANDY JOHNSON ONCE observed, "When you're playing with harder base-balls, and harder bats, and smaller ballparks, things like that, those are the intangibles that I think about as a pitcher." Well, the truth is he could have itemized a whole bunch of other factors that impact the pitching game, both positively and negatively.

It's not as if players from bygone eras didn't have it tough. Prior to 1884, pitchers were not permitted to throw the ball overhand. Then again, up until about 1910, usually only two baseballs were used per game. The ball became soft and scuffed and runs were scarce—imagine Johnson using such a ball nowadays.

All in all, there are some factors that pitchers have control over (at least to some extent) while there are others that they simply must live with.

Defense

Other than having the freedom to sign with the team of his choice when he becomes a free agent, a player has little or no say over the defense that plays behind him.

Jesse Orosco, who has pitched in more contests than any man ever, said pitchers not only rely on their defense, they respect their defensive players. And that can hold true even for a fielder who might make a lot of errors. For example, in 2000, Robby Alomar committed 15 errors, then an ungodly amount for him, but no pitcher would dream of suggesting Alomar was slipping.

Orosco realizes that many times a player who commits errors is a man with acres of range, a man who gets to a lot of balls that other guys can't reach. Most of his errors will be on the throwing end, often after making a dazzling stab of the ball. As for the occasional roller that gets through a fielder's legs—pitchers realize those thing happen, although rarely.

Orosco cited Rey Ordonez as being special because his errors are "on plays you could never imagine him [even] making, and then he tries to make an unbelievable throw and maybe throws it in the stands or something like that." He said pitchers respect such effort. When Mike Bordick played behind him in Baltimore, Orosco said his glove "saved [him] a number of times. That's how you win games—you have to have defense behind you."

Of course, nowadays defenses can be improved by working on the positioning of the players in the field. Sophisticated studies lead to scouting reports and myriad printouts, which lead in turn to subtle as well as drastic shifts at times. In the precomputer days, many pitchers kept a "book" in their minds as to where they wanted their defense to shade certain hitters.

Naturally, if a pitcher is a low-ball thrower such as a sinkerball specialist, he hopes he has four good gloves in his infield and a grounds crew that will keep the grass in that infield shag-carpet thick. Conversely, a pitcher who is up with his pitches had better pray for a fleet outfield contingency, wind blowing in, and a spacious home field.

Experience

Larry Bowa asserted that no matter what kind of skill a starting pitcher has, it will take him about three years' experience before he will start to live up to his potential.

According to Dennis Cook, "A lot of guys don't learn how to pitch until they're 30, 31 years old. I'm learning something every day." He spoke those words when he was 29, and was still pitching some 10 years later. Meanwhile, some experts pick a broader range for a pitcher's prime, from 28 to 32 years of age.

Feller said that in his youth he never really learned how to become a pitcher because, back then, there was no need. He commented, "I figured that even if I walked a few batters, I could power pitch my way out of a jam. By the late 1940s things were different. I'd lost a lot of my steam, and I realized I had to be a 'pitcher' out there, not just a thrower."

Another factor is that until a pitcher displays his ability and demonstrates control of his pitches, he will not be given borderline calls. In 1998 when Greg Maddux faced a promising rookie named Rolando Arrojo, who would shortly thereafter be named to the All-Star squad, Maddux got calls four inches off the plate. Meanwhile, the umpires squeezed Arrojo's strike zone. One teammate of Arrojo anguished that it was a case of "Maddux and the umpire versus Arrojo and the umpire."

As Lee Smith put it, "I think I hit that outside corner for about five years before they [umpires] actually thought I knew what I was doing. You have to gain respect, just like the hitters, from the umpires. I had no problem with that. If you go out there and throw a strike and you're going against Barry Bonds, you got to hit that corner a lot, you got to make good pitches. You can't throw a couple up on the screen and expect to get a pitch on the corner."

He said two pitches from the same hurler, hitting the same spot, will usually be called a ball against a Bonds, but a strike against a lesser hitter. "The guys who don't need any help, end up getting the help."

When it comes to endurance, Orosco is the ultimate survivor. He spent the bulk of the 2003 season as a 46-year-old, closing in on 1,200 appearances. A four-decade veteran, he was still around because he had fit a specialist role that had become so important—a southpaw reliever who can enter the game late to get one (sometimes more) vital out against a dangerous left-handed hitter. Usually that batter is Bonds, Shawn Green, Todd Helton, or Larry Walker.

Pitcher Allie Reynolds was succinct in his viewpoint on experience, saying, "You get smart only when you begin getting old." And manager Birdie Tebbetts pointed out that the difference between a veteran hurler and a rookie was just the same as that "between a carpenter and a cabinetmaker."

Normally, such observations hold true, but even a veteran can get rattled—perhaps even more so if he's in an important game. In the finale of the 1974 World Series, Dodgers great Mike Marshall entered the game and worked a scoreless sixth inning. However, when he went to the mound to start the seventh, he had to endure a six-minute delay when fans threw objects onto the field. Seemingly shaken by being thrown out of his rhythm, Marshall served up what turned out to be the game-winning homer to Joe Rudi on his first pitch.

Helping Your Own Cause

Another beneficial pitching component that has nothing to do with actual pitching prowess is how well a pitcher fields his position. Men such as Mike Mussina, Bobby Shantz, Jim Kaat, Bob Gibson, and Maddux were able to field their position with uncanny Gold Glove dexterity.

Leo Mazzone, somewhat surprisingly, said he didn't consider it crucial for a pitcher to field bunts or up-the-middle grounders, helping his cause with the glove in that respect. He preferred to see a "natural flow all the way through the delivery, because it takes pressure off your arm as you deliver the baseball." With his great pitching staff, he didn't care if the opponents earned a few cheap hits as long as his pitchers followed through, sometimes taking themselves out of the traditional fielding position.

The ability to hold runners on first is yet another talent some pitchers have. Runners may have taken liberties on Dwight Gooden and, more recently, Maddux, but they don't drift far off the bag against the likes of

Andy Pettitte. And through mid-September of 2002 and 31 of Kenny Rogers's starts, not one man tried a steal of second because of Rogers's excellent pickoff move.

Terry Mulholland, who has a good move to first base, commented, "Over the course of my career, I've managed to shut down the running game against me. It's helped me at this point in my career. As a reliever, I come into a ball game late and know that there's the potential for the other team to be stealing bases and getting guys into scoring position on me. It's a little bit tougher, [but] over the last 12 years I think I've given up nine stolen bases." That statistic is especially amazing in that he is usually called into a game with a man (or more) already perched on base.

Many lefties are notorious for baffling runners with their deception, some having balklike moves. Mulholland said, "Being able to throw strikes and keep them where they're at is a big advantage as far as trying to close out the game or at least set up to the closer."

Again, interestingly, Mazzone feels it is more important to focus on the batter and the throwing of a good pitch rather than fret about a potential base stealer. The aim is to get the batter out. Even if the runner steals and eventually scores, a big inning may be avoided if the pitcher concentrates on his main role: getting batters out. As Mazzone wrote, "one run in an inning will rarely kill you. Runners have taken some liberties with Maddux over the years, yet he remains one of the all-time greats."

Mazzone does work on having his pitchers develop a quick release and a slide step as methods of holding runners tight. He doesn't believe in "all the nonsense of throwing over too much" to first base.

Over the years there have also been a plethora of pitchers who "helped themselves out" by wielding a good bat. Top one-season totals by good hitting pitchers include: home runs, nine by Wes Ferrell; highest batting average, .433 by Walter Johnson; hits, 52 each by George Uhle and Ferrell (a total that projects to about 200 hits if they had batted as many times as a regular); and most runs driven in, 32, also by Ferrell.

Babe Ruth hit .304 as a pitcher and remains the last World Series starting pitcher to be penciled into a lineup spot other than the number-nine hole. In the 1918 Fall Classic he hit in the sixth slot during one of his wins and came through with a triple and two runs driven in. By the same token, the winningest lefty ever, Warren Spahn with 363 victories, hit the most homers as a National League pitcher — 35 in all, just 3 shy of the all-time mark held by Ferrell.

Meanwhile, in his perfect game, Catfish Hunter collected three hits. In Rick Wise's no-hitter, he won 4–0 while supplying three of the runs on two homers. Finally, in a 17–3 laugher, Tony Cloninger swatted two grand slams and set a single game record for runs driven in by a pitcher with nine.

For years Tom Glavine has, like a regular, taken extra batting practice. In 1996, when he won his second straight NL Silver Slugger Award as the top hitter at his position, he crushed the ball to a .289 clip. That prompted his hitting coach, Clarence Jones, to marvel, "He's got a good feel for the ball. Pitch him inside and he pulls it. Pitch him outside and he'll spray it to the opposite field."

Glavine commented, "Instead of being an automatic out, I figured my bat in the lineup could be a big advantage for me."

Pitchers must be aware that they can develop bad habits and tip their pitches. As portrayed in the hokey movie *The Babe Ruth Story*, during Ruth's pitching days he went through a stretch where pitchers seemed to know what pitch was coming — and, so goes the story, they did. It seems Ruth would stick out his tongue when he was about to throw his curve.

In a much more modern tale, in August of 2002 Colorado closer Jose Jimenez had to rid himself of a "telling" habit. He would hold his hands at the belt when he came to the set position prior to throwing a fastball, and would hold them chest high before dealing a change or slider.

Home Park

Three of Koufax's four no-hitters came in pitcher-friendly Dodger Stadium, and his lifetime won-loss percentage there was a staggering .818.

Billy Wagner stated, "There's parks that you feel more comfortable in, and I don't think it's necessarily because it's a big park or a small park. I've always felt comfortable pitching in Pittsburgh and in Cincinnati, but I've done just as well pitching in Enron [now Minute Maid Park] or at the Astrodome. And there's places like in L.A. and San Francisco that I've struggled in. I think it's just because of the [opposing] team, not necessarily the field." For one thing, he said he felt the mounds around baseball are not significantly different these days.

Trevor Hoffman is of the mind that a pitcher shouldn't let the ballpark influence his game plan. "If you get caught up in that, you're going to have some type of issue every place you go. I mean, you got a [hitter-friendly] Coors Field in our division, you got Pac Bell with the short right field, you got the big ballpark in Arizona [Bank One Ballpark], we know the ball flies there, Dodger Stadium is a good pitchers' park, so should you have more success there.

"You start getting caught up in that sort of thing then you're going to be a basket case out there. So, again, the only thing you can control is—not the outside factors of the ballpark, wind, fences, umpires—the only thing you can control is your ability to throw the pitch."

Palmer's book *Pitching* addresses the issue of pitching in various parks. He said that in Tiger Stadium and in Fenway Park he felt as if he couldn't afford to make as many mistakes due to the proximity of the outfield fences. The opposite was true in Yankee Stadium and in his home at Memorial Stadium in Baltimore.

Palmer said he naturally tried to keep the ball away from hitters in small facilities, but he wasn't afraid to try to fool a Red Sox batter who was accustomed to looking outside, with an occasional ball in.

During his first visit to Fenway, Satchel Paige had a one-sentence synopsis of the hitter-friendly facility: "Man, what a pitcher's graveyard." Shuey's view on the venerable ballpark is interesting in that he perceives a difference in visibility there between day games and night games. "Night games are consistent—you're going to have a real good view of the ball, but during day games, it's pretty consistent that they're not going to see the ball as well."

During his playing days, Smith observed, "The American League is a lot easier for guys to hit home runs. Guys who 'miss' the ball still hit the ball out of Tiger Stadium and Boston, places like that." Still, he said he didn't worry about what park he was in, be it his home park, a park with a short porch, whatever. He simply tried to focus on "just making quality pitches, that was the main thing. If you don't make quality pitches, they can hit them out on the road and they can hit them out at home. I tried to keep the ball down and move the ball around, keeping hitters off balance."

A benefit of such thinking is Smith was undaunted by the prospect of, for instance, throwing inside to a pull hitter at Fenway. "You can't just pitch a major league hitter one side of the plate. You've got to mix it up and take your chances. And these major league hitters now can hit a ball [pitched] away out, it doesn't really matter."

Years later, Shuey related to Smith, saying, "After you've been in Safeco [Seattle], Jacobs [Cleveland], some of these new parks, you don't like the old parks—you don't like going to Fenway. The tradition is there, but it's like you want to visit it, you don't want to pitch in it." The same could've been said of Ebbets Field, a locale Erskine said "was one of the toughest parks to pitch in."

Shuey feels that pitchers, who already have it tough with the lively ball, don't need the added stress of toiling in a bandbox. "If the game was the way it was back then, where pitchers were given a little more leeway here and there—the mounds were taller, balls were used more often so they were a little softer—shoot, you might like those parks a little better. But right now, you want them as big as you can find them, and you want as much room as possible."

Pitchers working in Pittsburgh's old Forbes Field didn't worry too much about giving up home runs in the spacious park. Singles would fall in all over the widespread outfield, but it generally took quite a poke to clear the walls. The deepest part of the park, for example, was a distant 457 feet away (for most of the park's existence). A batter almost needed a buccaneer's spyglass to see that part of the park.

Palmer also wrote that when the White Sox put in artificial turf, it hurt their team because their pitching staff featured lowball pitchers such as Tommy John, Joe Horlen, and Gary Peters. They would seduce hitters to smack grounders that might have been outs on a grass field, but scooted through the infield made of the slick artificial surface. The Sox, by going with turf, did the opposite of what many teams do when they tailor their park to meet their players' needs.

The turf infield also can be tough on pitchers since it holds so much heat. Palmer wrote, "the heat factor is something you can't escape." He said he seldom pitched in a park with artificial turf but did so in the 1970 All-Star game in Cincinnati. "I pitched three innings," he continued, "and I've never been so tired in my life." It was due to the humidity and the heat thrown off by the turf.

However, some field conditions can be controlled by the home team. Ryan Klesko said teams nowadays will still alter the field at times for that home field advantage. He gave an example of how the grounds crew might "water home plate down really big time if they've got, maybe, their sinker-baller going that day. That may be coming from the pitcher talking to the grounds crew. For the most part, though, it's pretty much the same thing [field conditions] every day."

The obvious advantage in Klesko's scenario is a sinkerball pitcher induces a lot of ground balls. By watering the area around the plate, the impact of the ball's initial contact with the ground is somewhat cushioned, so the ball won't whistle through the infield. Instead, it will slow down, becoming a routine groundout for the infielders and a very grateful pitcher.

Since Lou Boudreau wasn't the fleetest of shortstops, the grass at Cleveland Municipal Stadium around shortstop was kept high and soggy to slow balls down. However, around second, where the smooth, quick Joe Gordon roamed, the grass was cropped short and the infield dirt in his territory was packed hard. Once more: it's called tailoring the field to a team's best advantage.

Emotion is yet another intangible factor in baseball. Some fans think players, going through the grind of a 162-game schedule, can become stoical or immune to the applause of the crowd. However, Steve Karsay said that's not true. When he enters the game in a tight spot to the roar and support of the crowd, it gets him going.

He said, "There's no question, you get the adrenaline pumping in that type of situation. It's always nice to play at home in front of the fans because in a hostile environment on the road, it can get a little crazy." Players have been known to become rattled by an enemy crowd, as was the famous case when Darryl Strawberry reacted negatively to the jeering chant, "Darr-yl, Darr-yl."

So, a friendly throng is just another part of the home field advantage, along with the fact that when a player is at home he tends to eat and sleep better with home cooking and a familiar bed. Any comfort or encouragement is an emotional plus for players.

Left-Handedness

When a baby boy is born, nobody knows whether he will grow up to be a righty or a lefty, but it sure can help his path to the majors if he becomes a southpaw. Just as fathers of young hitters occasionally try to train their son to be a switch-hitter, fathers of potential pitchers should definitely pray that their boy will throw with his left arm. A left-handed reliever with the ability to face and retire an opposing lefty can last in the majors for a long, long time.

While only about 10 percent of the population is left-handed, the percentage of lefties who make it to the majors and who excel is disproportionately higher. In fact, a survey taken around 1990 revealed that about 20 percent of all pitchers are southpaws; by 2003 that figure had risen to around 27 percent. So while left-handers suffer many disadvantages in everyday life, they find it easier to win a spot on a baseball roster. In that same survey, it was noted that a whopping 60 percent of the pitchers who had attained the 300-strikeout total in a season were lefties.

In 2002, lefty Mulholland, then a veteran of 16 campaigns, said, "In the game of baseball, just like in mainstream life, the percentage of left-handed people is smaller than right-handers. Having a left-hander out on the mound is a luxury to some teams. I mean, you can look around to both National and American League teams and look at the number of left-handed starters compared to right-handed starters and you can probably count the left-handers on two hands.

"Given that, left-handed relievers are also a premium commodity and guys like Jesse [Orosco] and Dennis Cook, myself, we're going to come in, we're going to throw strikes, we've got experience on our side. And not only is it tough for a left-hander to face a right-hander, but sometimes it's a little bit too out of the ordinary for some right-handed hitters to face left-handed pitchers.

"So I think that's where it's tougher for right-handed relievers to stick around longer, because there are so many of them. You can get former starters, you can get lifelong relievers that are right-handed and everybody sees a right-hander just about every day whereas sometimes you can go a few days without seeing a left-hander."

While anybody who has played youth baseball realizes that, for instance, a 10-year-old left-handed hitter is at a huge disadvantage when he first faces a portside pitcher, Mulholland felt that advantage, to a lesser extent, still holds at the big-league level. "Especially for left-handed hitters with the ball moving away from them. It's a lot easier when you have a ball coming toward you. Most right-handed hitters have a little bit of a down-

and-in dominance as far as being able to hit a pitch down and in, whereas from a left-handed pitcher, you're not going to get that pitch very often; you'll get down and away, you'll get up and away, you'll get up and in, but very rarely do you get the majority of pitches coming down and in."

Umpires

Pitchers have virtually no influence over umpires. Other than trying to throw the ball in a given umpire's strike zone and avoiding getting that ump riled, there's little a pitcher can do in this realm.

Orosco, the graybeard of baseball in the 21st century, said that he doesn't tend to argue with umpires not only because he doesn't want to get on their bad side, but for other logical reasons as well. "Umpires have their set ways. I'm sure they're doing the best job they can. I know I've thrown pitches where I thought they were strikes, but I know if I go out there and start arguing I'm going to get away from my game. So I've got to respect what an umpire is doing."

Plus, he continued, "All umpires are different—some have a low strike zone, some are high. I watch games for the first few innings on TV [at the ballpark] to see what the strike zone looks like so I know what it'll be like during the game. So when I go out there I'm prepared. If [the strike zone] is the opposite of what I saw, I might say, 'Hey, what's going on?'"

Lately, experts such as Orosco have come to believe umpires seem to be squeezing the zone as the offensive explosion continues in baseball. It seems as if umps, who used to call the letter-high strike, now don't even give pitchers a strike at the belt. Orosco stated, "I just hope they don't squeeze it too much because it's hard enough right now. The hitters are really doing a number on pitchers."

During a 1998 interview when he noted the surge in the offense, he predicted that season would produce "about 20 guys with 40 home runs— you've never seen that in your career. It might take three or four years to get numbers like that. If they squeeze the strike zone the numbers are just going to go up higher."

He certainly got that right. Twenty men with 40 or more homers nowadays is hardly shocking. In 2000 baseball even set a new record for the most men with 30 home runs or more with 47 hitters reaching that plateau. And all *that* was before the Barry Bonds explosion.

Before umpires were consolidated, when a pitcher was traded to a new league he had to get used to a new set of umps and their strike zones. Smith said when he first moved to the American League, he tried to observe umpires' tendencies and chatted with his new coaches and teammates to glean such information.

Umpires are hardly infallible, and Smith recalled a time home plate umpire Charlie Williams got fooled by one of his pitches. "When I first started throwing the cut fastball, I threw a cutter and Charlie told me [that he had called the pitch inaccurately because] he was looking for a slider. I was like, 'What? Are you hitting now? You're going to start hitting back there now?'" Apparently instead of seeing the ball and calling it, Williams was anticipating what pitch would be on its way. Having never seen Smith's cutter, he was, like a hitter, handcuffed by it.

Weather

Smith said he also gave a great deal of consideration to the weather. On cold days when hitters' hands sting on contact, pitchers thrive. Smith commented, "In April in Wrigley probably I threw [only] five or six sliders; I tried to throw all fastballs the whole month. The hitters, a lot of the guys from Arizona to California, they weren't used to the [cold] weather. I mean, I would bust them inside, plus their timing wasn't right early in the season, so that had a lot to do with it."

He knew, too, that pitchers' hands don't respond well to frigid conditions or other inclement circumstances either but said it didn't faze him "because the rest of the guys had to play in it, too."

He said in his case he wasn't too concerned with the wind at Wrigley because he "threw sinkers. I threw a two-seamer and a four-seamer. So it depends on the hitter, the situation in the game, things of that nature, but if you keep the ball down in Wrigley—and they always had the infield pretty thick—there weren't too many base hits going through the middle."

As for other parks, he remained unconcerned about the direction of the wind. He wasn't one of those pitchers who, upon popping out of the dugout for the first time, gazed at the flag to check on the direction and speed of the breeze. He recognized that some lowball pitchers might feel that on a day with a stiff wind coming in they could afford to come up, or miss up in the strike zone a bit. However, he said he didn't change. "I stayed with the Lee Smith strategy—I was stubborn."

Scientists have studied such factors as the influence of wind patterns in various parks. Joe Niekro, for instance, said his knuckleball was helped out by pitching in the air-conditioned atmosphere of the Astrodome. He also liked the fact that the wind wasn't much of a factor on the movement of his pitches. If anything, knucklers like throwing with the wind blowing out, since it makes their number-one pitch dart around more than when the wind is blowing toward the plate.

Palmer added, "If the wind is blowing in, you realize you just have to throw strikes and not walk anybody. But if the wind is blowing out, you might try to pitch a little finer, be sure you make better pitches, maybe try to keep the ball down a little better." He compared that pitching strategy to what he did in a park with a slow infield—he'd focus on keeping the ball down.

Bert Blyleven liked pitching in Arlington Stadium because "the wind used to blow in from right field." He contrasted that facility to The Ballpark at Arlington, saying he doesn't like it as much simply because it's "more of a hitter's type of ballpark." The physical structure of the newer park has cut down on the wind factor, helping the offense.

The Mound

The height of the mound has influenced the pitcher's game throughout the history of baseball. In 1968, the mound was still 15 inches high and pitchers dominated the game, arguably, like never before. The next year when a rule lowered the height of the mound to 10 inches, home runs soared by nearly 50 percent.

Grooming the grounds to gain a home-field advantage is a part of the inside game most fans will never see. When Bob Feller pitched, he loved to throw off a high mound. Back then the rule about the height of the mound wasn't usually enforced, so owner Bill Veeck instructed his grounds crew to please Feller, making sure his ace was looming over the batters when he took to the elevated mound.

Some baseball observers have said that since the hitters are currently going through a productive period tantamount to the Renaissance, pitchers should be given an edge to offset the offense. The way fans love offense, it's surprising they haven't moved the rubber to the outfield side of the mound, forcing pitchers to throw uphill, but longtime coach Joe Nossek suggested baseball raise the mound. While he wouldn't go so far as to raise it back to 15 inches, he would take it up a few inches.

When asked about the idea of raising the mound, reliever Scott Stewart rather unexpectedly stated, "I don't worry about that. If that happens it happens. I'll 'worry' about it when it happens. I can't control that stuff, so I don't think about it." One would expect all pitchers would want the mound raised, but, apparently, some of them are focused enough to deal with what conditions they have and not concern themselves with off-the-mound matters.

If Glavine pitched against the Cincinnati Reds every single start, he would have loved it—until 2003, that is. He owned the Reds and loved pitching in their old park, Riverfront Stadium/Cinergy Field. By midseason of 2003, his 25 wins against the Reds were the most he had against any club. However, when he took to the rubber in their new facility, Great American Ballpark, he complained about the flatness of the mound, joining a list of others who felt the same way.

The Baseball

The quality of baseballs is now generally pretty standard, but over the years baseballs have been as mushy as a stewed vegetable and as lively as the proverbial rabbit ball. Even nowadays, though, a pitcher might reject a ball because he simply doesn't "like the way it feels." Some pitchers will ask for a new ball, seeking one with seams that are raised comparatively higher. This helps them get a grip on the ball and allows them to throw sharper curves. Dennis Cook has been known to upset other teams by rubbing the ball in an effort to raise its seams.

A major league baseball is supposed to weigh five ounces and be nine inches in circumference, but it may have a fourth of an ounce and one-fourth of an inch variance. Some pitchers will reject a ball that feels heavy to them, as they prefer a light ball, which tends to break (curve) more. Of course, others argue that a heavier, smaller ball travels slightly faster.

From 1876 until 1976 balls used in American League play were made by a different company from the one that provided balls for the National League. Writer Martin Quigley said the balls used by NL pitchers had seams that favored curveball artists, while the AL baseballs helped pitchers who relied more upon their fastballs.

Baseballs used to be softer, and Shuey noted that in the days of long ago a scuffed ball stayed in play longer than today. That, he said, meant "when a guy [got] jammed, it stays in the park."

Most pitchers today feel the balls being used since the mid- to late 1990s are lively if not out-and-out juiced. They used to call such baseballs "rabbit balls" since they hopped off the bat. Pundits used to say the method of testing baseballs was to put a stethoscope to the ball. If it was a rabbit ball, one could hear a tiny, rapid heartbeat from within.

Genetics

Heredity is yet another element of the game. A pitcher's bloodlines can help him immensely. Justin Speier feels his strong arm was a legacy from his father, former big-league shortstop Chris Speier. Likewise, Satchel Paige was blessed with a durable arm. In 1965 at the estimated age of 59 he worked three innings and surrendered no runs in a big-league contest, impressing none other than future Hall of Famer Carl Yastrzemski. No man ever pitched in the majors at an older age.

Unpredictability

Another pitching intangible came from Michael Barrett, who said that sometimes a pitcher benefits from being "effectively wild and [doesn't] even come close to hitting the target." This works to a pitcher's advantage if he isn't too wild, too often. Sometimes a hitter might be guessing where the pitcher is going to work him. A hitter will quickly give up such tactics if the pitcher is wild. Imagine a batter looking for a pitch away only to get buzz bombed by a tight fastball. Therefore, at times, even a factor such as unintentional wildness can be a tool of a pitcher.

Teamwork

Sometimes if a pitching staff features two excellent pitchers, the competition between them will spur both of them on. Curt Schilling said that was true of his relationship with fellow Arizona ace Randy Johnson. "Being in the presence of someone who pitches at that [Johnson's] level, you have some pride. You certainly try to match or measure yourself up that way," Schilling told *Baseball Digest*.

Then again, many pitchers will help fellow pitchers out. Erskine would arrive early to the Brooklyn locker room and talk with teammates. Erskine recalled, "I'd talk to Preacher [Roe], 'I'm having trouble with Sid Gordon. How do you pitch to him?' It was a sort of game prep on a personal basis.

"We'd hold our [pregame] meeting to go over hitters in the open area of the clubhouse. Normally the starting pitcher was right there in the middle of the meeting saying, 'Here's how I'll pitch to [Alvin] Dark, and here's how I'll pitch to [Willie] Mays.'" Pitchers would not only learn from one another, but such meetings were (and still are) held to reveal how pitchers planned to work hitters so the defense could react accordingly.

Mulholland said that while pitchers and hitters are traditional enemies, when a given hitter is a teammate, pitchers will share insights with him. A pitcher might, for example, tell a hitter what went through his mind when he pitched to him in the past, revealing some details about how he likes to start the batter out. Who knows—ultimately the information may enable the batter to help the pitcher win an extra game or two.

Mulholland commented, "Yeah, but nobody says you have to give away all your trade secrets. I'm all for helping my teammates for the good of the team but there are some things you want to keep in your back pocket. I know, for instance—I've been traded enough times in this game, I've faced plenty of former teammates and you're going to face them so you got to get them out somehow, you don't want to be telling them exactly what you're going to do."

Which brings up the age-old question: do hitters or pitchers have the advantage when they face a former teammate? Mulholland replied, "I think the pitcher has more of an advantage because you can sit in the dugout and you can watch another pitcher pitch to a teammate of yours and see how he gets him out and see what he hits and never have to face him. Then, when you go out on the mound, he's never seen you from the mound and yet you've seen how all the guys have pitched to him and gotten him out.

"Obviously, he's been in the field while you've been pitching, and maybe seen your approach, but as a pitcher you've got *x* number of different options as far as what kind of pitch you can throw, where you can throw it, and how hard you can throw it."

Expectations

Expectations placed on a highly touted player can actually impair his performance. Jaret Wright made an impact soon after reaching the majors, most notably with his victory in his first World Series start, Game 4 versus the Florida Marlins. It was then that he became the second-youngest pitcher ever to start the deciding game of a World Series. For that matter, he was just the seventh rookie ever to get the starting nod for the seventh game of the Series.

Cleveland manager Charlie Manuel thought that all the hype later hurt him. "It raised everyone's expectations so much. He was not a finished product at the time. When he pitched in the postseason that year nobody had seen him. For a short period of time Jaret got by pitching the way he did, but then he had to change." Some pitchers can't make the change and subsequently don't succeed.

Durability

Some pitchers seem to be injury-prone, while others go forever without putting in any downtime on the disabled list. Chan Ho Park had gone six healthy seasons with the Dodgers, missing just one start. Then, in

Texas, he had gone on the disabled list twice by his first August there. The second inactive stint was due to nothing more than a blister on the middle finger of his throwing hand. Clearly, health is a fickle but crucial matter.

Atmosphere

Although one would expect highly paid big-leaguers to be focused all year long, staying motivated is not an easy task. If a pitcher's team is, say, 20 games out of first in early August, it's simply a matter of human nature for some personality types to pull a Fido act—rolling over and playing dead. In contrast, a pitcher's intensity during a pennant drive is at a peak, which does enhance his performance.

Shortly after pitcher Jeff Fassero was traded to a contender one year, he said of his new team, "It's just the atmosphere here. You get complacent when your team is mediocre. You go about your business kind of side-stepping. It's good when you've got something to work for. You're a little more excited when you come to the ballpark."

Dominance

Finally, a strange phenomena: in baseball jargon, a pitcher who dominates a particular batter is said to "own" that hitter. When one studies all the incredible records Babe Ruth carved into the books, the impression is that he "owned" the entire pitching staffs of the American League. He not only hit for power with his 714 lifetime homers, he also crushed the ball at a lofty .342 clip.

Keeping that in mind, imagine this scenario: The year is 1922 and an obscure pitcher is toeing the rubber against the Yankees at the Polo Grounds under the Roman Coliseum facade. His gaze falls upon the looming figure of Ruth in the batter's box, just 256 feet away from the inviting target of the right-field fence. Remarkably, instead of being intimidated, St. Louis Browns pitcher Hub Pruett goes right at Ruth.

Further, he'd soon learn that he had little to fear in future duels as well; Ruth was *his*. Throughout his career, Pruett would completely baffle the "Babe." Later, looking back on his first confrontation with Ruth on April 22, 1922, Pruett said, "It didn't bother me, facing Ruth for the first time. All I knew was that he batted left-handed and I didn't have much trouble with left-handers. When I went out to the mound, I didn't know who he was. I struck him out on three pitches."

Indeed, it was no fluke—the 21-year-old rookie southpaw continued to oppress Ruth. During Ruth's first 13 tries versus Pruett, he tapped out to the pitcher, drew two walks, and struck out an abysmal 10 times. In fact, of his 21 plate appearances in 1922 Ruth whiffed 13 times, an unbelievable 62 percent of those futile trips to the plate.

Pruett only lasted three years in the American League, where he'd face Ruth 30 times in all. Ruth hit a paltry 4 for 21 (.190) against Pruett with just one homer. He struck out in exactly half of their battles, leading Pruett to say, "Seeing the Babe strike out was almost as exciting as seeing him hit a home run."

Ruth's lone homer versus Pruett came when the pitcher did not go with his best pitch, his fadeaway. Pruett wanted to throw it for an out pitch to Ruth, but his catcher, Hank Severeid, shook Pruett off and, said Pruett, "called for the curve. I hung it and Ruth hit a line drive over the low right-field wall [in St. Louis]."

Pruett's key weapon against Ruth was a rather uncommon pitch in those days. Modern terminology has changed it to a screwball. "It's just a reverse curve," said Pruett. "I don't think he [Ruth] ever hit my fadeaway.

"When I was a small boy, my baseball idol was Christy Mathewson. Matty's most famous pitch was the fadeaway. When he threw it, the ball would break in on a right-handed hitter and away from a lefty. I got to thinking if a righty pitcher like Matty could throw it, why couldn't a lefty like myself do it?"

He did, developing three ways of throwing it: overhand, underhand, and three-quarters. Such a variety of releases helped him dominate Ruth, but his lifetime slate was a mere 29–48 scattered over seven seasons. Pruett spoke to Ruth only once in his life. As players they "passed each other without speaking. But every once in a while Ruth did something that gave me a kick: he would wink at me," said Pruett. Many years later, about two months before Ruth's death in 1948, the two adversaries met at a baseball dinner.

Pruett approached Ruth and said, "If it hadn't been for you, nobody would ever have heard of me." Ruth replied in a raspy cancer-stricken voice, "That's all right, kid, but I'm glad there weren't many more like you or no one would have heard of me."

All-time great Lee Smith experienced a similar situation. He said that "the one guy who probably hit me the best was Ron Jones." Amazingly, Jones was, compared to Smith, a stiff, lasting only four years in the majors where he had only 65 hits. "It seemed every time I threw him a pitch, he hit a double off me some place or other. He had about two months in the big leagues and got, like, five hits off me," Smith chuckled.

Jones apparently was so comfortable against Smith, one would expect Smith would've hit him with a pitch. Smith just laughed, "I was trying to get him out *one time* before I started hitting him. He was on base every time I was throwing, [so] I was just trying to get the sucker out."

He said that he did brush him back, but even that failed: "He hit a double. I dropped him. I had him 1-2. I said, 'I got to go inside.' I went inside, dusted him off, and came back with a forkball on the black; he slashed it right down the left field line. I was like, 'This guy's seen everything.' I was making up pitches. I threw a changeup, I was turning over a screwball, [pitches] I didn't even have; I was making them up as I went along." That's the point it came to for the frustrated Smith.

How does a pitcher figure out such an occurrence? He conceded, "I have no idea. Certain hitters just pick up the ball better. I also had trouble with Pittsburgh, and I'm not talking about Barry Bonds and Bobby Bonilla, I'm talking Curtis Wilkerson and Tom Foley and Lloyd McClendon, when those guys came in there after Barry and Bobby and Andy Van Slyke and those guys were gone."

12

Secrets of Select Pitchers

Steve Carlton

PETE ROSE SAID that the great pitchers such as Carlton would almost always throw their best pitch with two strikes. Many pitchers agree, saying, "Why work the batter's weakness? I want to attack him with my very best weapon." So, even though some gullible hitters might look for a Carlton fastball on, say, a full count, he would throw his "out" pitch, his sharp-as-a-straight-razor slider.

Carlton introduced his version of that pitch in 1969, the season in which he set a record with 19 K's in a game, after having struggled the year before. Adding one new pitch, and perfecting it, helped enormously.

According to writer Nathan Aaseng, Carlton also had the ability to obliterate extraneous factors from his mind. Whether facing a Hank Aaron or a Rose, Carlton focused only on the plate and the catcher's mitt. "No one," said Carlton, "can hit well off me if I'm doing my job." So, to him, the batter's identity and tendencies were incidental.

Then there was his famed exercise program that included stretching, lifting, and martial arts work. The single most publicized aspect of his training was probably the exercise in which he'd plunge his arm into a rice-filled tub, clawing and clutching at the rice while working his arm as deep into the tub as he could. It sounded easy, but those who tried to match "Lefty" found it impossible to master.

Roger Clemens

The Rocket, like so many great pitchers, has many secrets relating to his ability. He once said, "I'll do anything I have to do to win. It's easy for me to stay focused on what I have to do. I just won't let things stand in my way." And that includes not merely such basics as working hard and studying the enemy, but also throwing tight to and/or hitting opposing batters.

"Clemens would be at the top of my list [of greats]," said Lee Smith. "I played with him in Boston. I had never seen a man work as hard as he did—even on days off and days before he was pitching. You think now he works hard because he's 39, 40 years old. He did the same thing when he was 23, 24, and you can look at his stats and see how that works for him."

Winning 20 in 2001 at the age of 39 is testimony to Clemens's durability. Incredibly, he still lit up radar guns in the low to mid-90s at an advanced age and did so with precision pitching. Not only that, he was among or even atop all strikeout artists in his league, not giving in to age.

Finally, a huge asset to Clemens is the wide array of pitches he can rely on. He has, of course, a two- and a four-seam fastball, a hard splitter, a slider, and a changeup to boot.

Bartolo Colon

In 2001, an American League scout told USA Today/Baseball Weekly that Colon was an ultimate power pitcher. "I've never seen anyone like him. His velocity actually increases as the game goes on." Colon has been known to cruise through a game with a fastball in the mid-90s. Then, suddenly, and almost inexplicably, he has been known to find a sort of second wind in the eighth or ninth inning.

Hitting instructor Clarence Jones explained quite simply that Colon "gets stronger as he goes [deeper into the game]. In the late innings he's throwing 100 mph. I can't see anybody having any better arm than him."

A scout said he also admired Colon's four-seamer that approaches 100 mph, and observed that Colon can then come "back with that two-seamer in the low to mid-90s. He has also learned to throw that two-seamer to lefties that runs across the plate and gives guys fits." His two-seamer tends to start outside before tailing back over the plate. Armed with such speed, Colon is unafraid to challenge hitters with fastballs.

Perhaps more important, it seems Colon has begun to learn how to pitch. In 2000, he averaged 17.2 pitches per inning to retire the sides. By 2002 he had it down to a career low 15.2 pitches per three outs.

Further, in the spring of 2002 on the advice of a coach, Colon began to position himself more on the center of the rubber. That change helped his control and displays how even a minute alteration can impact pitchers.

Even though it's been said that it takes longer for fastball pitchers to develop than others, Colon makes it look almost effortless.

Former teammate Shuey said simply, "He throws as hard as I've seen anybody ever throw. I know [Bob] Feller threw amazingly hard and that's what Bartolo does right now."

Don Drysdale

One batter said of "Double D," only half-jokingly, "The trick with him is to hit him before he hits you."

Drysdale's very delivery was frightening. At 6'5", he would come at hitters from the side, throwing hard and anywhere he wanted. He felt that he, not the batter, owned the plate. Perhaps his most famous quote on his style of pitching was: "If one of our guys went down [on a knockdown pitch], I just doubled it [decking two enemy hitters]. It didn't require a Rhodes scholar . . . I had to protect my guys." In return, they gave a fierce loyalty to Drysdale.

Another great line indicative of his philosophy was: "The pitcher has to find out if the hitter is timid. And if the hitter is timid, he has to remind the hitter he's timid." Needless to say, with Drysdale the reminder that he delivered was never a gentle one.

Dennis Eckersley

Former relief pitcher Rob Dibble, a member of Cincinnati's Nasty Boys cadre of pitchers, said what made Eckersley the best in the game was the fact that "he's got style. The thing I like about him is that he challenges everyone. He's not afraid of anybody. He comes in the game and says, 'No one can beat me. I'm the best.'"

Dave Duncan, Eckersley's pitching coach for years, told *Beckett Baseball* that "Eck is very good at knowing who likes to swing at the first pitch. He's capable of throwing it just off the plate. The umpires respect Eck's knowledge of the strike zone and sometimes give him that pitch."

In the same 1991 article Eckersley added, "If I had stayed a starter, I probably wouldn't have achieved this level of success. If I hadn't developed the forkball, I'd probably be out of the game."

He also told *Baseball Digest* that Tony LaRussa's moving him from a starter's role to that of a one-inning closer was a blessing. "When I started, my first inning usually stank. As a reliever, I had to get into it, I had to just let it fly."

That's exactly what he did—working fast, throwing strikes, and doing so with outstanding control. Over a three-year period he walked just 16 hitters over 206 innings.

Bob Feller

Feller, sometimes called "Rapid Robert," made his big-league debut in 1936 as a 17-year-old. In that start, the future Hall of Famer blew it by 15 batters and came right back in his next start with 17 K's. Shortly after that, he returned to high school to complete his senior year. "I didn't know much. I just reared back and let them go. . . . Sometimes I threw the ball clean up into the stands," said Feller of his early days with Cleveland.

Like Ryan, though, that wildness was a plus in that not many players want to dig in on a guy who throws hard and at times doesn't know exactly where the ball is going to go.

By the time he was a mere 23 years old, Feller had won 109 contests and had three 20-win seasons to his credit. Able to hit 100 mph, he recorded three no-hitters and once set down 348 men on strikes in a season.

Bob Gibson

The definition of intimidation is Bob Gibson with his cap tugged down over his eyes—eyes frozen in a perpetual glare. He'd make batters quiver with his blistering fastball and wicked slider. He was cool on the hill and clinically cool in lecturing on hitting batters. "I hit guys in the ribs," he said. "The ribs don't move."

Gibson, like Sal Maglie, did not like to get to know his opponents as people. "Even at All-Star games, I didn't talk to anybody except pitchers," Gibson told *Boston Globe* writer Gordon Edes.

He also told Edes another secret of his—learning to pitch around effective hitters. Gibson, who once posted a 1.12 ERA, gave the example of Billy Williams and how the Cubs outfielder hit Gibson hard. "That's [facing a Williams] when you can't be too stupid. Swallow your pride. Use your better judgment. Pitch around somebody."

He also helped himself with a fine bat, and, like many pitchers, was quite proud of his hitting. He once boasted, "They pitched to me as they would a hitter, not a pitcher. I *was* a good hitter."

Tom Glavine

Glavine is the type of pitcher who knows both his and his opponents' strengths, but he also tends to disregard a given batter's forte if that is

Glavine's strong point, too. In other words, in a given situation Glavine may well throw a slider to a hitter who hits them well.

At one point in his career Glavine even dumped his curve for a considerable stretch because, while it was nice to have four different pitches in his repertoire, the curve wasn't really helping him, nor did it show signs of improving back then—it simply wasn't a good pitch *for him* at that time.

He is able to get by with a fastball that nears, but seldom touches, 90 mph, because his changeup, which he can spot inside or out, is so deceptive. Plus, he can toss in adequate sliders and even an occasional curve. Given the fact that he can also throw a sinker when needed, he is truly hard to solve; his assortment keeps hitters guessing and off balance. He is further known for working batters away, avoiding the meaty part of the plate.

All in all, says Kirk Rueter in *Sports Illustrated*, "He's the guy you want to pattern yourself after if you're left-handed and you don't throw 95."

A durable pitcher, when he developed a sore elbow in June of 2003, there was talk of him having to go on the disabled list. In his entire 16-year career up to that point he had never spent a minute on the DL, and he had almost never even missed a start. In fact, when he did miss a turn on June 11, it was his first missed start in 11 years.

By 2002 he stood number nine on the all-time win list for southpaws. Another factor of his success is his ability to adapt. In 2002 he began to throw to both sides of the plate more than he had done in the past.

Goose Gossage

Although Gossage said he never consciously took to the mound trying to be intimidating, the net result was the same. He was a great reliever, in part, due to his style.

He stated, "I mean, when you throw 95 or better, and I'm all arms, legs, and I'm not looking at the hitter—I never got a good look at the plate—my delivery was very intimidating. They couldn't pick the ball up; I'd hide it very well. It was a combination of those three things, I think, that really made me successful.

"It was never an act for me. My demeanor on the mound was always natural. I felt like a Jekyll and Hyde. When I went between the lines, something snapped in me. The hitter was the enemy."

Gossage confessed that he had "hit a few guys in the head, but never intentionally." Of course, that's not much consolation for those men's aches. They would probably grumble, "Who cares if it was an accidental beanball? It still hurt."

He also said that it takes a lot of energy and effort to stay intimidating over the years. In 1994, at the age of 43, he observed that he, somehow, managed to "get pumped up, but I don't know that I'm as intense or as intimidating as I used to be." Hitters, no doubt, would have said that he was just as menacing as ever.

"Goose Gossage was an idol of mine," Lee Smith freely admitted. "I used to admire him in the bullpen. I'd get in there and I'd throw the ball as hard as I could to the plate and turn my back on home plate like he did."

Trevor Hoffman

Hoffman is the master of the changeup, making him rather rare in that most closers (with exceptions such as Doug Jones) rely upon heat to put out the fire—a truism even though it appears, on the surface, to be paradoxical.

Did Hoffman ever have doubts or fears about throwing slow stuff to major league hitters who might tee off on his offerings? He replied, "I think any type of pitch that you have that's referred to as an equalizer pitch, that's an out pitch—strikeout type of pitch, I think it's always set up off your fastball. So there's no difference in me—you locate your heater, you get ahead, and then you show them something they haven't seen."

Hoffman chuckled, recalling the old line about Jones throwing "slow, slower, and slowest." He said, "I saw him pitch and there was no doubt that he had three different speeds and all three were probably under 85. But Doug was the master of changing speeds and keeping you off balance and had a long career with it.

"We've discussed some things; I had the opportunity to meet him in Arizona. He lives in Tucson and I went to school there and at alumni games we had a chance to talk. My changeup definitely evolved from talking to other guys," said Hoffman, revealing the importance of learning from older, experienced, successful pitchers.

To further illustrate, he added, "I threw a circle change and then a guy came over [to the Padres] in the Fred McGriff trade in '93, a guy by the name of Donnie Elliott, that held it a little bit different. So it kind of evolved a little bit more and then to be able to get a little more velocity off of it, I went to 'choking' it [holding the ball deeper in the palm of his hand]. It helps to talk to other people."

Interestingly, in an age where most scouts are looking to add some giddyap to pitches, Hoffman found success by slowing his out pitch down. Now he compares his pitch to "more like a palm ball than it is like a straight change.

"It definitely would be nice to have the ability to rear back and throw it by guys, but even so, early in my career that was the case, but I'd get hurt with location. So, location is more important than anything else, I think."

Although Hoffman once could throw in the 95 mph range, it's said that his changeup is so smooth and deceiving, hitters mistake it for his fastball. That's how badly their timing is off, not unlike the occasion a pitcher by the name of Bugs Bunny fanned a brawny cartoon batter on a single, tantalizing, superslow changeup. Paul Lo Duca also had a colorful comparison when he told *Sports Illustrated* that Hoffman's changeup looks "like it has a parachute on it."

Being lucky enough to stay healthy can be another factor for a pitcher. Of course, health can, in part, be attributed to working out and staying in good shape. Either way, through 2002, Hoffman, the first reliever ever to rack up 30+ saves in eight consecutive seasons, had never spent a day on the disabled list throughout his 10-year stint in the majors. Unfortunately, he went under the knife twice after the 2002 season, freezing him in the number-five slot on the all-time save list.

Hoffman, who has only one kidney, was a failure as a minor league infielder. As a matter of fact, when he became a pitcher, he hadn't pitched in a game since his Little League days. So, his perseverance also has paid off.

Through 2002, he was able to convert almost exactly 90 percent of his save chances, the best clip since such records were officially kept, starting back in 1988. Further, his best single-season conversion rate is an even more astounding 98.1 percent in 1998—the year he compiled 54 saves while blowing only one.

Randy Johnson

If Johnson were a quarterback, he'd be the strong-armed Brett Favre, capable of throwing a strawberry through a brick wall.

Billy Wagner can hum the ball pretty good, but when he was asked to name the fastest pitcher of them all, he replied, "Randy Johnson by far." His reasoning was this: while there are relievers such as himself who can hit 98-plus on the radar gun on "a particular pitch for two innings, he's still doing it in the eighth and ninth inning" in games where he's already thrown tons of pitches.

On August 25, 2002, Johnson retired 16 via strikeouts en route to a shutout. The Diamondbacks' radar gun recorded a 102 mph fastball on a strikeout that ended the seventh inning.

His manager, Bob Brenly, pointed out another Johnson "secret" when he said, "He's maximizing every bit of his body." At 6'10" it's to be expected that he'd get a whole lot of leverage out of his frame, and he certainly does.

Still, a huge factor in his success was when he added tools to his arsenal beyond his normal 95–100+ mph fastball. He throws two types of sliders, one that catches the outside tip of the plate, a "backdoor" pitch, and one that comes low and tight to righties.

Outfielder Michael Tucker told *Baseball Digest* that Johnson's slider is so devastating he had "seen guys swing at it when it's about to hit them in the back foot. You're talking about some just ugly swings on that pitch."

Johnson, aware that today's sluggers lean out over the plate, has said that pitchers must keep those hitters off the plate by busting them inside. He refuses to let hitters dig in—armor, as is commonly worn now, or no armor.

Johnson's former Arizona manager, Buck Showalter, told the *Phoenix New Times* that hitters always look for something tempting to swing at.

However, when it comes to Johnson, they seldom get an offering that makes them feel they could do much with the pitch. Showalter also called Johnson so durable he would still be up in the 100 mph area even after throwing as many as 120 pitches.

Power pitchers seldom last the way Johnson has. Case in point: through 2002 only he and Nolan Ryan had logged six seasons of 300-plus strikeouts.

Walter Johnson

There is a famous, *perhaps* true, story about a time Ray Chapman faced Walter Johnson. When the count got to 0-2, Chapman is said to have turned to the ump and muttered, "You can have the next strike; it won't do me any good." He then pivoted and trudged back to the dugout.

Early in his career one observer said of Johnson, "He throws so fast you can't see 'em." Then he added that it was a good thing Johnson had sharp control, "because if he didn't, there would be dead bodies all over."

Johnson himself summed up his mastery over hitters when he coined the phrase, "You can't hit what you can't see." His fastball was that impressive and that intimidating. It's unfortunate that his career was spent with the hapless Senators who played in Washington, known as being "first in war, first in peace, and last in the American League." Had he played on a good team, there's no telling how many contests he would've won. As it was, he captured 417 decisions, second only to Cy Young's 511.

Billy Koch

Brian Moehler evaluated Koch back in 1999, beginning by saying, "Koch is phenomenal. The things about him are he seems to have a pretty good idea of the strike zone for a young kid. It's not just rear it up there and throw it, he can put in on the corner when he needs to."

Back then, Koch, in his early twenties, had already displayed a sizzling fastball, but Moehler felt he deserved as much or more credit for his tenacity. After injuring his elbow, Koch underwent Tommy John surgery. While many pitchers need about a year and a half for recovering, Koch was back on the mound in half that time. Not only that, he was back to firing 98 mph fastballs with regularity. Moehler said, "He came back throwing harder than he ever had. He's hit 100 mph [in 1999]. Wagner [usually] flirts with 97 to 99, but Koch, I tell you, he can bring it up there!"

He is also armed with a sinker, slider, and a curve. Further, as the cliché goes, he wants the ball. He craves being on the hill when the game is on the line, and that applies day in and day out. In 2002, for example, he worked close to 100 innings, leading his league in relief innings pitched.

Sandy Koufax

In 1963 Koufax, at 27, went 25–5 while posting a minuscule ERA of 1.88. Yogi Berra commented with incredulity, "I can see how he won 25 games. What I don't understand is how he lost 5." Actually, after his first six seasons, Koufax had a mediocre lifetime ledger of 36–40 even though he had signed as a bonus baby in 1955. Nowadays the only thing "baby" about his bonus would be the size of it—reportedly a paltry $15,000 to $20,000.

Early bouts of wildness had led him to consider quitting the game. He lamented that even when he "finally got the ball over, they'd hit it." Before total desperation set in, though, Koufax pleaded for a few more chances to take to the hill. His general manager, Buzzie Bavasi, reportedly barked, "How can you pitch when you can't get the side out?" Koufax retorted, "Who can get the side out sitting in the dugout?" Faced with that rebuttal, Bavasi gave him the opportunity to get some starts and the move paid off.

Another reason Koufax was finally able to undergo the transformation from being merely a struggling pitcher armed with potential to superstar status was the help he got from catcher Norm Sherry. He instructed Koufax to throw his curve and changeup more often while taking just a bit off his blazing fastball to gain the control he so drastically needed. Those changes allowed Koufax to become a pitcher, not merely a thrower. When all those factors clicked, he was so hard to succeed against that

Willie Stargell noted, "Hitting against Sandy Koufax is like drinking coffee with a fork."

Then, too, Koufax said he improved a lot as he began to become a Rodin-like thinker on the hill, saying he "learned to concentrate on the next pitch and forget about the last one." After his 1963 no-hitter, manager Walt Alston concurred with Koufax, commenting, "He always had good stuff, but the last two years he has had good control to go with it. He uses good judgment and now mixes up his pitches."

His curve was not only sharp, it also moved to the plate as if controlled by a missile directional system. One reporter gushed that Koufax was "overpowering with his fastball and he cut the corners with his curve."

Former teammate Carl Erskine, who had a fantastic curve, admired Koufax's breaking ball. He called it "a big, rotating, classic curve." Koufax had one thing in common with law enforcer Eliot Ness—they were both untouchable.

Still, he often would rear back and go with the hummer. When he engineered his 1965 perfect game, his last obstacle was Harvey Kuenn. "I gave him all fastballs, and I gave it everything I had. It worked," remarked a fatigued Koufax after racking up his fourth no-hitter in as many seasons.

Finally, in Leonard Koppett's *Thinking Man's Guide to Baseball*, Koufax was quoted as saying, "I became a good pitcher when I stopped trying to make them miss the ball and started trying to make them hit it."

Greg Maddux

Cliff Floyd of the Marlins was asked what it would take to build the ideal ballplayer. He replied, "Barry Bonds's wrists, Vladimir Guerrero's arms, . . . Cal Ripken's health, and Greg Maddux's brain." The unassuming Maddux manages to go about his job with the determined yet quiet self-assurance of Peter Falk's Columbo.

Interestingly, not everyone has always touted Maddux as being a great pitcher. Lee Smith recalled the time when the Cubs "said Maddux [listed at 6', 185 pounds] was too little; it makes you ask, 'What are you guys thinking?' It's one of those things where those [smaller] guys had to prove themselves. [It was as if Maddux had to say], 'Hey, I'm just as good a pitcher [as others] with just as good of stuff and longevity as some guy that's 6′3″, 220.'

"Him and Jamie Moyer, that's all I ever heard about, that they were too little. I thought, 'Man, they're not going to run the ball across the plate.' And now you see both of those guys are still doing pretty good," he said, using understatement intentionally.

Maddux's secrets include the fact that he is aggressive. Even though he's a control pitcher and not at all overwhelming (usually topping out in the high 80s), he goes at hitters, having faith in his stuff and, of course, his superlative control. His repertoire, including a sinking fastball and another over-the-top fastball, as well as a cutter and a fine changeup, keeps hitters off stride, as does his backdoor movement.

So, clearly there's more to pitching than merely speed. Jon Saraceno of *USA Today* quoted Boston scout Matt Sczesny as saying, "You take a Greg Maddux and put the gun on him and, jeez, he's no prospect at 87, 86 [mph]. But he doesn't throw a ball that's straight. It's about command and movement."

One of Maddux's former catchers, Eddie Perez, elaborated on that observation, saying that Maddux throws his fastball "over the top, but his ball moves a lot. He throws sinkers and cutters to both sides of the plate — that's what makes him so tough to hit."

Not only that, Smith added, "He's the only guy that I see who can throw a backdoor fastball. I think, 'How do you do that?' But he's still doing it."

He gives hitters nothing to salivate over and is unafraid to throw a strike on, say, an 0-2 count, as he does not like to waste pitches. In fact, in 2002 he led his league in least amount of pitches spent per start.

In addition, other attributes are his stinginess in surrendering home runs, his sheer will and determination, and his fielding prowess. Through 2002, he owned 13 consecutive Gold Glove Awards.

In Tony Gwynn's *The Art of Hitting*, the San Diego star elaborated that Maddux "isn't the most overpowering or intimidating guy, but he has great movement and great location. Maddux just never gives you anything to hit. He just keeps changing speeds and painting the corners. It makes for a long day." He felt Maddux was a challenge to face, adding it was never easy to get "a real good swing on the ball of a location pitcher."

Arizona slugger Luis Gonzalez spoke on the topic of Maddux, saying, "Are you talking about Picasso? That's what I call him. When a guy can throw the ball where he wants to, anywhere, on any pitch, at any time in the count, that's painting. And no one paints like Maddux."

One-time Houston manager Larry Dierker continued the laudatory comments, "I love watching this guy, especially on TV, because he carves up hitters like a surgeon. As a pitcher, the most important thing is location. The second most important thing is the movement of the pitch. The last thing is velocity. Well, he has two of the three.

"But you can ask any of our guys, and they'd tell you they'd much rather face a guy like [Mets closer] Armando Benitez who throws 98 mph and has no idea where it's going than this guy."

Meanwhile, Glavine told *Sports Illustrated* back in 1985, "I think he's got a gift. He's able to notice things in the course of a game that no one else can—the way a hitter may open up a little, move up in the box an inch, change his stance." Many pitchers rely on their catchers to catch such subtle changes; Maddux counts on himself.

In 1994 when the entire National League had an ERA of 4.21, Maddux matter-of-factly recorded a microscopic 1.56 ERA, a monumental accomplishment, leaving all other pitchers behind in his dust.

Noteworthy, too, is the fact that when Maddux struggled at the start of the 2003 season, he felt umpires' strike zones were shrinking on him. "In the past," he stated, "if you threw 10 borderline pitches, 5 were called strikes and 5 were balls. Now maybe 9 are called balls and 1 a strike." Despite occasional obstacles, he has endured and is an all-time great.

Matt Mantei

In his finest years Mantei was virtually untouchable. His fastball topped out around 97 mph, and league batting averages versus him were typically way under .200. In 1999, his 13.64 strikeouts per nine innings was bettered by only two relievers. That year one scout labeled him "the best of all the up-and-coming arms in baseball."

Despite the fact that he endured back and rotator cuff surgeries, Mantei was a very effective and intimidating pitcher. Perhaps one of his biggest "secrets" was his willingness to throw his great fastball in tight to anybody.

The key to his career is not his speed or "stuff"—those are givens—it's simply maintaining his health.

Pedro Martinez

In a 1998 interview, Mo Vaughn was quoted in *USA Today/Baseball Weekly* as saying that it seems like Martinez "doesn't even have to use all his pitches all the time. He seems content to go with his fastball and changeup until he has to make a tough pitch with the slider." What a luxury it must be for Martinez to be able to save such a pitch, pulling it, magician-like, out of his Red Sox hat when necessary.

In the same issue of that publication, Martinez's catcher at the time, Scott Hatteberg, observed, "He pitches like a finesse pitcher—but with overpowering stuff. He is easy to catch because he hits his spots so regularly."

When Lee Smith was with Montreal, he was a teammate of the 5′11″, 180-pound Martinez. Smith recalled, "I think Pedro actually thinks he's about 6′9″ and about 240. He pitches like that because he's aggressive and he uses both sides of the plate. He doesn't let the hitter get comfortable up there. He moves the ball in and he makes good pitches.

"He's a hard worker also, but I think he got bent out of shape a little bit early in his career when everybody was labeling him as being too little. 'Oh, he's not big enough, he can't do this and he can't do that.' He showed them that he could do it. That's one thing I like about him—having to prove somebody wrong with the stuff that he has is unbelievable. It's amazing how hard that man can throw a ball and with good movement. The reason the Dodgers got rid of him was they said he was too small."

Smith said it's possible Martinez began throwing tight as another way of proving himself to others. Then Smith added, with a knowing laugh, "that and the fact that he doesn't have to hit, that helped a little bit."

However, it should be noted that even in his young days in the non–designated hitter National League, Martinez insisted that he made his living throwing tight to hitters. He said no matter the repercussions, he wasn't about to change.

Perhaps another reason he plunks batters from time to time is, as Smith observed, "because he has so much movement on that ball—it's live, man. And I don't think he's actually throwing *at* guys, but you can't let a hitter dive [at the ball]. Half of these guys got all the body armor and they're diving, covering the whole plate. A pitcher has to have one part of the plate. I mean, if a hitter's going to hit the fastball in *and* the fastball and breaking balls away, then there's nowhere for me to make my money, you're not going to be around that long. You have to have one side of the plate, but I don't think you have to hit somebody in the head or chest.

"If you keep the ball down and you brush somebody in or hit them in the backside or the thigh, they don't mind that—they respect that." The problem occurs when pitchers go up by the chin or even throw behind a batter, and Smith commented, "I know Pedro and I don't think he's the type of person who would actually try to hit somebody in the head.

"But you've got to come in tight. It sends a message plus it lets a guy know, 'Hey, you can't cover both sides of the plate.' That's a pretty good message to send and I think they heard it."

Respected hitting instructor Merv Rettenmund said that against the great pitchers, a hitter should be at the plate ready to attack the first good-looking fastball offered. Easier said than done against a Martinez, a man with precision control and a vast assortment of pitches, each one as good as the other. Rettenmund added, "If you let Pedro Martinez throw a fastball away for strike one, then that means you can hit his changeup; and I'll tell you what, Tony Gwynn can't hit his changeup, so I know that no one else in baseball can hit it. So, you're done; you're a dead man right now."

Martinez is so superior, hitters rely on hyperbole to describe him. "I hit a foul ball off Pedro and I was happy. I could hear the crowd cheer," said Sandy Alomar Jr.

Travis Fryman said that at one point, "My wife told me I've got 17 strikeouts in 23 at-bats against Pedro. I'm a major league hitter. I've faced the best pitchers in the game. I ought to be able to put the ball in play half the time."

When Russell Branyan was with Cleveland, he was asked to list the various starters who have the best fastball, best slider, and so on. He didn't even have to go pitch by pitch, he simply said, "Probably Pedro's got the best everything. Pedro doesn't throw a split, but his changeup is more effective—he's got an awesome changeup and breaking ball."

Christy Mathewson

One of the five charter members of the Hall of Fame, Mathewson had several huge secrets to his success. As a right-hander, he had a pitch that was called a fadeaway, a slow pitch that broke in on right-handed hitters, making it a mirror image of the screwball that lefties throw. However, he had a wide selection of pitches, including good fastballs, curves (back then his curves had colorful names such as the outdrop and the dropball), as well as a changeup to augment his fadeaway.

In fact, since the fadeaway was so tough on his arm, requiring a reverse twist of his wrist, he threw it only about a dozen times a game, saving it for prime spots. Indeed, it's been said that the only pitcher who relied on one main pitch as physically demanding on the arm as the fadeaway was southpaw Carl Hubbell, with his famed screwball. It's also been noted that after throwing that pitch so often, his wrist faced outward at all times—as though he had mutated himself by countless twists of his wrist.

Meanwhile, Mathewson won so many times (373) because his control was simply phenomenal. In 1905 he won all three of his World Series starts on shutouts and did so while issuing only one walk over 27 frames. In addition, he once went 68 consecutive innings without giving up a free pass.

Mathewson once said there was no such thing as his "best pitch." He felt that any pitcher's best pitch is the one the hitters aren't teeing off on during a given game. "If they start hitting my fastball, they don't see it anymore that afternoon. If they start getting ahold of my curveball, I just put it away for the day. When they start hitting both of them on the same day, that's when they put me away."

Jamie Moyer

Moyer can afford to get away with his slow stuff due to his fine control. He mixes things up and moves the ball around so the batter doesn't see the same pitch in the same vicinity two times in a row, keeping hitters way off stride.

Additionally, he is patient and won't give in to batters. Even when he falls behind to hitters, he still pitches his game, never aiming the ball or giving in to the hitter and grooving a fastball.

Plus, according to accepted baseball wisdom, pitchers like Moyer who work fast and keep the ball around the plate tend to have their defense play more alertly behind them, knowing the ball may soon be hit their way. Slow-working pitchers sometimes see their defense playing flat-footed, almost bored by the tedious pace of the pitcher.

Smith said that he was really surprised with Moyer's success, but it was because in his youth as a Cub "he had trouble at Wrigley [Field] because of the changeup being his out pitch. I don't think his career would have been near what it is now if he had tried to stay in Chicago because there a pop-up is in the bleachers. But he's showed them that he still has good stuff."

The Cubs organization didn't respect Moyer's soft-stuff style (and Maddux's lack of a scorching fastball). "We had a kid, a highly touted left-handed pitcher named Drew Hall—they thought more of that guy than they did of Moyer and Maddux. They thought Hall had a better chance of being the better pitcher because he was a big lefty and he was throwing 93, 94." Hall, by the way, went on to post a 3–4 record with Chicago.

Phil Niekro

Most experts agree that Phil Niekro is the greatest knuckleball pitcher ever. His career win total of 318 is not only the highest for knucklers, but, through 2002, ranked thirteenth all-time for *any* pitcher. His secret is, of course, his elusive specialty pitch, taught to him by his father.

However, unlike many knuckleball pitchers, Niekro had more tricks up his sleeve. His off pitches, while not devastating, were effective enough to keep hitters honest, more so than any other knuckleball hurler ever.

In fact, the day Niekro racked up his 300th win, he felt he had something to prove to the baseball world. He wanted to show that he could win without his renowned knuckleball. So, he took to the hill against Toronto on October 6, 1985, and breezed through the first eight innings, taking a 8–0 shutout into the final frame.

It wasn't until the last batter, former MVP Jeff Burroughs, stepped up that Niekro broke his vow. With two outs and a count of 1-1, he decided he simply had to put the final batter away via his money pitch. Two pitches, and two strikes later, Burroughs had struck out and Niekro had fittingly recorded his 300th big-league win.

"I always wanted to pitch a whole game without throwing a knuckleball, because people thought I couldn't get anyone out without doing so," said the maestro of the pitch after his historic, nearly knuckleball-free win.

Fittingly, the man who has tricked more hitters than anyone ever with the knuckler was born on April Fool's Day of 1939. Since then, he frustrated many a great hitter—including Pete Rose, who was once asked what it was like to face "Knucksie." He commented, "Hitting Phil Niekro's knuckleball is like trying to hit a butterfly." Dick Allen put it another way: "I just take my swings and go sit on the bench. I don't even want to mess up my swing."

Jim Palmer

The all-time Orioles great had a lot going for him, but one overlooked asset was his uncanny ability to rarely give up homers with a lot of men on base. Solo homers don't hurt great pitchers as much as mediocre pitchers because a Jim Palmer would usually work around the solo shot and find his way out of other jams, finishing a game with his low ERA intact (his lifetime mark was 2.86, trailing only a handful of men). A three-time Cy Young Award recipient, he lasted 19 years, won 268 contests for Baltimore, pitched 3,948 innings, and never once surrendered a grand slam!

In *The Ripken Way*, Cal Ripken Sr. complimented Palmer, who played for him in Aberdeen in his first year at the professional level, for his willingness to listen to advice. Ripken noted, "Jim was very intelligent when he came into professional baseball, and that didn't change over his entire career. He had an idea of how he was going to pitch to the hitters on a ball club before he even took the mound."

Palmer said he got the majority of his outs on high fastballs, especially when he'd first get ahead in the count, then begin working the hitters up.

Rettenmund got a chance to appreciate the team's marvelous pitching staff. He liked Dave McNally as one of the best he played with or against from the 1970s era. "He didn't have great stuff, but he had the command." However, naturally, Jim Palmer was the elite of the O's. "He was different because he had *really* great stuff.

"Before the game, he knew every pitch to every hitter. He was as well prepared as Greg Maddux. Palmer knew every hitter on the other club and the pitches he would throw. He's the only pitcher I've ever seen to walk the bases loaded [while] throwing a no-hitter to get to the one guy he had to get to.

"It was against Kansas City and he did that in the ninth inning to get to him." Rettenmund said that he was positive Palmer did it intentionally. "You got that right! Jim Palmer *walking* three guys in an inning?! And he never gave up a grand slam in his *career*. He knew [that day] the only pinch hitter Kansas City had left and he got to that guy to throw the no-hitter. Now, is that preparation or what?!

"Jim's the only pitcher I've ever seen who didn't want to sweat; go out there and get the inning over on three pitches." He was also, like Maddux, clinical in his approach to the game.

Rettenmund concluded, "If you had to win a game, I would probably take him out there any day of the week."

Troy Percival

Like some hitters who crave a java jolt, Percival says he drinks about 10–12 cups of coffee before and during each game. However, a more important ingredient to his success, he says, is his knowledge of how to pitch, and the ability to somehow get by, even on days when he doesn't have his best stuff going for him.

When Percival was young, he had a role model, which also helped his career enormously. That person, Lee Smith, was ideal because he employed the same basic style as Percival and had been through the travails of the bullpen.

In 2002, when Percival led the league in percentage of converting saves (91 percent), he notched seven postseason saves, relying on sheer heat quite often. Still capable of hitting 100 mph at times, his typical fastball scorches at 95–98. It's no wonder Steve Karsay said that of all the veteran relievers around with great velocity, he was most impressed with "Percival's fastball out of the bullpen."

When Percival mixes in an occasional curve that is around 20 mph slower than his fastball, hitters mumble, "It's just not fair."

Gaylord Perry

Mike Cubbage, a longtime player and coach, recalled a great Perry tale. "When the Texas Rangers traded for Perry, Jim Fregosi walked up to Gaylord to greet him. He handed Gaylord a small tube of Vaseline and asked him, 'What's this?' Gaylord looked at him for a moment then said, 'That? That's a two-hit shutout.'"

Actually, though, Cubbage revealed a Perry secret: "Gaylord was more of a K-Y jelly guy."

At times, though, Perry would deny the existence of that pitch. Once, after his retirement, when asked straight out to talk about the spitball, Perry replied, "That's the pitch they thought I threw—I never did." Of course, in his autobiography, aptly titled *Me and the Spitter*, he admitted he'd load one up in crucial situations.

Perry even joked, "I'd always have [grease] in at least two places, in case the umpires would ask me to wipe off one. I never wanted to be caught out there without anything." Then he added ironically, "It wouldn't be professional."

On a serious note, Perry also said of his best pitch, "I changed speeds on it and used it as a good off-speed pitch."

Perry said he always wanted to finish what he started, not trusting his fate to the bullpen. In 1972, the year he won the Cy Young Award, he started 41 times and worked deep enough into the game to earn 41 decisions (24–16 with a save). By the way, in a different era Grover Alexander set the record with 48 decisions in 48 outings.

Dan Quisenberry

Tekulve elaborated on the secrets to Quisenberry's greatness. "He kept the ball down, was very consistent in keeping the ball down, and, like most of us [submariners], had good movement, and the ability to throw every day."

Both pitchers could make the ball move in different ways besides down. Teke went on to say, "Yeah, you could change it, just depending on how you released it—whether you change your wrist angle or how you put the pressure on your fingers. You can change the movement.

"It becomes such a thing that you develop a feel with the baseball and you could almost, in your mind, decide which way you want it to go, what you want it to do. Do I want this one to sink, more down? Do I want this one to run more away? And you have a feel for it where you can just kind of let the ball go and it will do that."

He said that unlike muscle memory, "it's just kind of understanding what's going on—why the ball moves in a certain direction, because it's spinning a certain way against the seams and you just got to understand what it's all about. You know which way to make the seams rotate to make it do what you want it to do." A lot of that comes with experience and "a feel thing."

Mariano Rivera

Going into 2002, Rivera had a record 24 postseason saves. In 1998 and 1999, over 25⅔ innings, his postseason ERA stood at an invisible 0.00. Furthermore, until Game 7 of the 2001 World Series, he had a streak of 23 save conversions.

Rivera throws a cutter that can hit 90 mph and, because his motion is so fluid, the ball seems to jump on the batter with jack-in-the-box suddenness, startling hitters as if they were infants. The effect is much like a strobe light: one flash and the ball's in his hand; then, blink, and it's in on the hitter. Also, his cutter runs away from righties, making it an evasive pitch. With left-handed hitters, the pitch tends to saw them off on their fists. Like Maddux, he doesn't rack up tons of strikeouts, but does induce countless harmless grounders.

Karsay praised Rivera's range of 92–96 mph. "His ball moves and cuts," he said, then added by way of comparison, "I think he has a very good fastball, but Paul Shuey has a split that's about 92, and that's about as filthy as it gets. His splitter is probably the best I've seen. An average guy throws it 82 to 84 mph and a good one goes 87 or 88."

Still, Shuey himself deferred to Rivera, praising his exploding fastball. He stated that the speed alone on Rivera's pitches, however, isn't the key to his success. "It's just hard to hit. He doesn't have many pitches; he's just got the one pitch, but he gets people out with it all the time. I probably throw a harder fastball than he does, but his is more effective. [So] he's got a better fastball than mine."

A key to Rivera's success, said Shuey, is, "He's got such a nice, easy, relaxed motion that when it comes out, it comes out on top of you. Whereas mine looks like I load up. His is sneaky fast."

Meanwhile, from the hitters' point of view, Robbie Alomar pointed out one good thing, perhaps the *only* good thing, about batting against Rivera: "He's a reliever so you don't face him a lot." Alomar added, "He's nasty."

Kenny Rogers

Rogers began to improve as a pitcher when he developed a good curveball to go with his fastball. Pitching coach Claude Osteen, like Rogers a lefty, helped him with that project while Rogers learned how to throw an effective changeup on his own. When all those factors gelled, Rogers had transformed from a thrower with no idea of what he was doing on the mound to a true pitcher with a plan every time he took to the hill.

If Rogers is in a situation in which he knows the batter is trying to hit, say, a sacrifice fly, or has the hit-and-run sign, it "changes it [the way he pitches] a little bit. I think the most basic point is you have to stick with what you know you can do because when the pressure's on, and it's a tight situation, you gotta know there's something that you can draw on—that you have the confidence that you can make the pitch and execute it at that time. And it's usually something that's your strength; you can't really try and rely on a weakness, like your fourth-best pitch or something like that, in a situation that you're not comfortable with. So you're going to go to the well that you've gone to before."

Further, in his case, he's gone there with all the success of a Texas oilman with a different type of lucrative well. Yet this perfect game performer admits he took a long time to learn his trade, especially the lesson of *not* trying to throw the ball by guys. Just how long did it take him to be cerebral on the mound? "Longer than most," he lamented, "but it's probably the biggest adjustment you make as a pitcher. Your stuff is there; I mean, we talk about it all the time in the locker room or wherever."

He said if only he could have known about 10 years earlier the insights he now has he would be a better pitcher "in every aspect, but it's just not the cycle; it takes the experiences, the successes, and the failures to where you learn. It just doesn't come [that easily]. I mean, the guys that get it early, they're the superstars. The guys who get it in the middle or later still are great players, but it's just something that doesn't come to everyone that quickly."

Now, as a veteran, he says that "without a doubt" it's a bit frustrating that he can't simply make a Xerox copy of his experience and his insights and pass it on to young pitchers. To do that would help his team's success vastly. "But it's going to happen at its own pace. You can't try to make it happen any quicker because it won't take. There's going to be a time when you're ready to open up and you hit the wall—you've basically gone as low as you can get, like, 'I gotta try something different.' It's hard for a young guy to go out there and try something different that they're not used to or don't have any confidence in."

As for one of his own early moments of gestalt or that magical "aha!" realization, he said, "I remember in the minors, Double-A, I had a pretty good arm, threw pretty hard, and I remember going out there one day feeling like I was throwing as good as I've ever thrown, as hard, and throwing strikes, too. I was feeling unbelievably strong and after the second inning, I looked up and it was 8–0, and we were losing. I didn't understand it.

"Well, the next day I sat in the dugout and watched an old veteran pitcher go out there and carve these same hitters up that, the day before, previously, wore me out. And he didn't have half the stuff I had, but he knew how to pitch. He knew how to change speeds and he used his head out there instead of a situation of when you do get into a jam, just trying to go harder. Going harder is not the way to be successful for most people."

He said it is "big time" difficult to learn the lesson of taking something off one's pitches. That perhaps holds true more now than ever in this age of radar guns, an era in which, again, a crafty pitcher like Doug Jones or Stu Miller might not even get a chance to sign a professional contract.

When asked to list his vital rules or secrets to pitching, Rogers responded with a chuckle, "Oh, gosh, that's not an easy question to answer real quick, but for me, like I've said before, you get out there and you see so many guys with great stuff but they don't know how to use it. Nowadays, you don't overpower hitters; it's just not something you can consistently do. You try and stay within yourself and pitch, and learn your mechanics to where you can duplicate them time after time after time."

Nolan Ryan

Ryan was as cool as the inside of a covered bridge. The confident Texan was not to be messed with—just ask Robin Ventura, who dared charge the mound on Ryan, only to be rebuffed by a barrage of blasts from the legendary right hand of Ryan.

He could intimidate with his fastball, no doubt. Still, take away Ryan's money pitch and he still had two highly effective pitches—his wicked curve and a changeup that moved a great deal. Another secret to his effectiveness is that he disguised those pitches so well, hitters had no prayer of knowing for sure what was coming. And, of course, even if they did know what to expect, they couldn't touch his stuff.

Former catcher Jeff Torborg had the honor of catching Nolan Ryan. He knew, therefore, firsthand how special Ryan was. "When you talk velocity, Nolan threw the hardest," he asserted. "Nolan threw it down the strike zone harder than any human being I ever saw. In 1973, against the Boston Red Sox, Nolan threw a pitch a little up and over my left shoulder. I reached up for it and Nolan's pitch tore a hole in the webbing of my glove and hit the backstop at Fenway Park."

Ryan commented on his wildness, a facet of his game he learned to deal with, saying, "It doesn't matter how many you walk so long as they don't score."

Long ago, traditional baseball thinking dictated that pitchers simply did not lift weights. In *Nolan Ryan's Pitcher's Bible*, Ryan wrote that he used a 12-station Universal gym, ignoring the theory that lifting would leave him "muscle-bound." He found that "even if I was somewhat stiff from lifting, it really had no effect on my ability to pitch. And after I began using the weights consistently, my arm would bounce back more quickly from one start to the next." Around 1974, Ryan also began to realize how important proper stretching and flexibility are for a pitcher, especially for preventing injuries.

Ryan wrote that when he was with Texas and part of a five-man rotation, he would "perform my lifting on the first and third days and usually ride the bike the first three days after a start." Such preparation and conditioning, he said, enabled him to pitch over 900 innings during his first three seasons in the American League.

Finally, he was also a thinker. When he authored his sixth no-hitter, the 23-year veteran said, "I was concentrating in the ninth just on making good pitches. I didn't want to make a pitch I'd second-guess myself. If they got a hit, they were going to get it on a good pitch." Normally that meant a fastball, but he also bent a few knees with his curve that night en route to racking up 14 strikeouts.

Curt Schilling

When Andres Galarraga was asked what pitcher gave him fits, he readily came up with the name of his nemesis: "Schilling. Why? Because he's got great control, he throws the ball where he wants it. He throws hard with good speed. [He has a] good slider, good sinker. I mean it's really tough to [track] him—he throws in different locations all the time."

Schilling is, of course, one of the most successful pitchers on today's big-league scene. One reason is his unique approach to his craft, including having the proper attitude. "I plan to get every hitter out three, maybe four times [each game]. Then it's a matter of execution." In other words, it's all a matter of if he can "make it happen," and he often does.

Mark Grace, a Schilling teammate on the D-backs, said the great righty, with his vast repertoire of pitches, has the makeup to be a big-game, go-to guy. "To beat him," Grace stated, "you have to hit him. He doesn't do anything to beat himself. He doesn't walk people. He holds runners on . . . You either have to get three hits in an inning or take him deep."

Grace, of course, was correct about Schilling's assets. On August 21, 2002, Schilling was in the midst of a truly fantastic season. Even though he was 21–4 at that point, his most sensational stat just might have been this: he had walked fewer men than he had won games, with only 20 walks issued. That's something rarely done for an entire season. Christy Mathewson did this twice with a personal best in 1913 when he won 25 while walking only 21 men.

In 2002, Schilling worked 259 innings, fanned 316, while surrendering a mere 32 unintentional walks, good for nearly a 10-to-1 ratio.

Schilling is known for quickly jumping ahead of hitters, often by firing an unhittable first-pitch fastball. Not only that, but when teams try to attack his first pitch, they often make quick outs and Schilling breezes through such games with low pitch counts. Almost ironically, teams that try to work Schilling deep into a count instead find themselves worked deep into a dismal 0-2 hole.

He is highly professional, evident from the extent of his preparation. Perhaps more than any other big-league pitcher, he scrutinizes video. He realizes how vital his planning is, saying that without it, "There's no way I'd be the pitcher I am today." While he agreed that a pitcher is expected to do his homework, not everyone is as diligent as he is. He makes a science out of studying his opposition, the way Ted Williams made a science of the study of enemy pitchers.

In fact, thanks to modern technology Schilling can select any major league batter and watch himself face that man on video. He likes to analyze how he has matched up against hitters for every single at-bat at his disposal. By 2002 he had amassed a library of nearly 100 CDs crammed with "footage" of every pitch he had thrown over the last five years, covering some 22,000 pitches—and his archives continue to grow. He can, and does, break down confrontations numerous ways, including by ball-strike count, the type of pitch he has thrown, the locations of his pitches, and more.

For instance, Schilling said it is vital for him to know which umpire will be working the plate on the day he gets his start, and even *that* can be analyzed. He has the ability to study every umpire in the game. Further, due to that scrutiny, he knows which umps call the most strikes, which ones, on the other hand, have the tightest strike zone, which will give you the outside corner, and so on. In that way, Schilling knows their strike zones thoroughly down to the percentage of pitches each calls for balls.

All this information is stored on his laptop and has been there since he began his study in 1996. He is still employing the basic program he used then. "Why add toys," he reasoned, "if I'm not going to use them?" He realizes that the software he does have is as powerful as it is vital.

What he uses on the days of his starts are the videos, studying them intently for 30 minutes to two hours before he "kind of finalizes everything."

Tom Seaver

Seaver had the knack of working hitters by throwing, for example, a high fastball followed by a curve down and then going back to a strike up high. Palmer followed a similar pattern at times with a variation—he'd get a hitter to chase a fairly high fastball and then work him "up the ladder." That is, Palmer figured if the batter chased that high ball, why not work that weakness again, but a little higher up? If the batter was lured into the trap again, why not tempt him with yet a higher offering? In the days of Palmer and Seaver such tactics worked. Now, with a lower strike zone being enforced, this may be a lost secret of pitching.

Seaver felt a pitcher has three elements to work with on the mound. He mentioned speed, hitting spots, and ball movement, adding that, to him, the least vital was velocity.

Charles Nagy said some of Seaver's secrets to success included "longevity—he took really good care of himself. He was a power pitcher; he had really good mechanics—he used his legs real well, drove toward the plate." As far as intangibles, Nagy pointed to Seaver's "desire—the desire and the heart to take the ball; a bulldog-type mentality where he would go after the hitters [with] 'Here it is, hit it,' type of stuff."

Lee Smith

Smith listed what he felt were the secrets to his greatness. "The main thing, as a relief pitcher, is you have to have a tough skin," he chuckled. "And when things don't go your way, you go back out there and give it your best shot—you don't go out there thinking about what happened yesterday. You like to get it right the first time, but I think knowing that I could play day after day made me tougher.

"As a starter, you go in there and you get beat up one day, you might not even see that team again and you gotta sit the bench for a week before you can play again. I liked being able to go to the ballpark knowing I got a chance to play, to go back out there every day."

In fact, he said that he got his first shot at being a closer because he was a rare power-pitching reliever who not only wanted the ball daily, but could handle the rigors of throwing as many as four consecutive days.

In addition to a great fastball, Smith said, "My second-best pitch was my slider and my forkball." Seldom throwing curves, he relied on "mostly sliders." He could even, at times, throw his fastball and slider from the sidearm slot, but that was just a different look as he normally threw the ball from a three-quarters delivery. He recalled with a deep laugh announcer Milo Hamilton describing his sidearm ventures, with humor mixed in with respect: "Big Leroy, throwing from El Dorado."

Since Smith is so big and threw so fast, he seemed very intimidating on the mound. Friendly off the field, he confessed that as part of his job, he would brush people off the plate. "Yes, I did, but it was tough for a guy being a closer to do that. You hit a guy, and then you got the tying run on base. I think, for retaliation and things like that, it was easier for starting pitchers, but if the situation comes, I don't really think that you had to hit a guy to get your point over. If you throw that ball in tight and get a guy off the plate, then you get respect. There are some times when you got to hit guys, but you don't want to end anybody's career."

While Smith and other closers have gained much admiration, he has to wonder why the Hall of Fame, through 2003, accepted only Hoyt Wilhelm and Rollie Fingers into its pantheon. Why not the all-time save king? Smith ruminated, "So many guys say, 'Oh, the closer only had to pitch one inning.' Well, Bruce Sutter pitched a few more innings than one." So, of course, did Smith during a time when that was more commonplace. "There aren't very many teams that would be World Champions without a good closer. Without Mariano Rivera, I don't think the Yankees would have had that many."

Smith was aware that some voters don't like to honor first-time nominees, so he gracefully shook off the initial denial. "Not too many pitchers in general got in on the first ballot, I understand that. I didn't have any problem with it." Many voters seem to prefer to go with players with big offensive numbers and "the guys that play every day."

Still, Smith can reflect with the same pride and calm dignity that helped him on the mound when "some of the guys that I played with and played against respect me." He's heard them say, "Smitty was one of the best players I played with." Further, he said, "That means a lot to me. But even to be thought of in the same breath with Hall of Famers like Babe Ruth and Hank Aaron and all those guys. I was like, 'A little country boy came from a graduating class of 26. I think I'm doing pretty good even to make it to the big leagues. I never dreamed I'd save 400—I didn't think I'd *play* in 400 games.'" Had he pitched under today's save rules for his career, he might well have rung up 500-plus saves instead of his final total of 478.

John Smoltz

The wicked-throwing Smoltz feels one secret to becoming a good pitcher is experience, something he says you can't teach. "Very few pitchers can come up and dominate like Dwight Gooden," said Smoltz back in 1991. "Everybody has to go through it. The fortunate ones win, while the unfortunate ones lose and learn from losing." So, even losing (but not *too* often) has some merit.

Smoltz is a rarity, a man who has won the Cy Young Award but now has become a closer par excellence. Over his last 49 appearances of 2002 his Braves lost exactly no ball games.

Even at the age of 35 he was still firing the ball around 98 mph, with his slider complementing that fastball because, at about 88 mph, it looks and acts like his fastball. However, with late movement, hitters flail at the slider and Smoltz just keeps rolling along, racking up saves with the same consistency as he had recorded victories.

Rick Sutcliffe

"He's another pitcher I really like," said Lee Smith, "a good teammate of mine, and a good hitter. He worked hard and he educated himself about the hitters a lot. That's what I liked about him. Half of the time, we'd be sitting on the bench together watching that other team hit. I really like his work ethic.

"Like I said, he was a smart pitcher. I just liked the way he was smart about how he was going to pitch a guy. I used to sit in on his meetings with him and [catcher] Jody Davis and talk about the whole lineup. He was educated to how he was going to pitch to the whole lineup before he went out there. I liked that and thought about him as, 'Sutcliffe goes between the lines, he's prepared.' When I go out there [in relief of him], I want to be prepared because he works for three hours and I don't [want to] come out in 20 minutes and screw it up.

"Really, he had a good overpowering fastball and a good curveball, he had pretty good stuff. But I think his mechanics, his delivery sort of screwed up so many hitters. He sort of hooked the ball behind him in his delivery. He had this sort of hitch where he stopped in there and the hitter [is] trying to time the pitch, and then the pitcher stops, then the hitter's got to get started again."

Warren Spahn

Spahn, the winningest left-handed pitcher of all time, accounted for his success quite simply: "A pitcher needs two pitches—one they're looking for and one to cross them up."

Spahn may also have been one of the most quoted lefties ever, too. He incisively cut to the heart of his craft, coming up with this gem: "I never throw a ball down the middle of the plate. In fact, I ignore the 12 inches in the middle and concentrate on hitting the 2½ inches on each side or corner of it." Of course, that comment also captured yet another of his secrets to pitching—the uncanny ability to spot the ball where he wanted it. For a southpaw to have that kind of control was simply amazing.

Then, too, there was his durability. Not only did he endure 21 seasons, he also "took the ball" every time a manager offered it to him. "Spahn hated to miss a turn," said one of his teammates. "He expected to pitch every fourth day no matter what. He loved baseball, and he loved to pitch; you got the feeling sometimes that pitching was his whole life."

Kent Tekulve

One of the most durable pitchers ever, "Teke" threw in an unconventional style for aeons. "Basically, ever since I was a kid when I played catch with my dad in the back yard as a nine-year-old or even before that," Tekulve began, "I threw the ball naturally sidearm. It was always something that I did. It was that way all the way through high school, college, and, actually, my first three seasons in professional ball.

"Then when I got to the Double-A level, I found out that I was having trouble: the ball was moving real well when it was around the strike zone, but not *in* the strike zone. I tried to figure out something to do to get the movement that I wanted in the strike zone.

"[At first], I did what everybody else does, I went up to the conventional three-quarters and that was absolutely useless; I had no velocity, no movement, no anything. Then I remembered, growing up in Cincinnati, there was a guy by the name of Ted Abernathy who pitched for the Reds when I was a kid. I went back, as memory would serve me, to a kid's vision of Abernathy and started trying to mimic that. That's where I kind of developed my delivery with the submarine.

"I found out that when I went down there, I got the movement that I wanted, and I actually threw a little bit harder from the lower slot. So, I started with what I remembered of Abernathy, started with that, and through trial and error, over the course of about a three-year period, I ended up coming up with what was eventually Kent Tekulve."

Further, what became Tekulve was a pitcher who kept the ball down, got good movement on the ball, and racked up outs with pool-hall precision. Even if he knew an opposing hitter was a sucker for high pitches, Teke kept shooting the knees. "I was always a believer in 'I do what I do best,' and if there's somebody that I can't get out that way, then I pitch around them and get the next guy."

Fernando Valenzuela

Valenzuela was like a knuckleball pitcher in that he threw a specialty pitch, a screwball. Now, that is not to say that he unveiled his secret weapon, the "scroogie," as often as a knuckleball artist throws his elusive pitch, but since both pitches are so rarely seen by big-league hitters, the pitch is as unique as it is difficult to hit.

Valenzuela, a southpaw, was certainly not the first pitcher to be armed with a screwball. Christy Mathewson, as a righty, threw a pitch that broke the opposite way of a curve, too. And, as mentioned, Hubbell was the original master of the screwball. The reverse twisting motion of the wrist required by this pitch is not only abnormal, it can be downright painful.

In Valenzuela's case, any discomfort was worth it as he broke onto the big-league scene in 1981 with an 8–0 record, including eight complete games. The sensation he caused, dubbed Fernandomania, swept Los Angeles and the entire baseball community. Few people realize, however, that his fantastic rookie season would never have occurred if scout Mike Brito hadn't discovered him. He's the man known for his savvy along with his ever-present white Panama hat and his constant presence behind home plate at Dodger Stadium armed with a radar gun.

That discovery took place in 1979 and can be chalked up to good fortune and to a good scouting department. Furthermore, another key was the Dodgers having pitcher Bobby Castillo work with a young Valenzuela. Castillo was the one who taught him the screwball, and it took Castillo only a few days to get the lesson across to a very apt pupil who wound up being much better than his tutor.

Another part of Valenzuela's success was the fact that he could help himself with the bat. In his first 15 big-league at-bats, he banged out seven hits. Dodgers announcer Vin Scully shook his head and muttered, "Is there anything this kid can't do?"

Billy Wagner

Brian Moehler said that as early as the late 1990s Billy Wagner showed "all the potential in the world," and had already become "almost unhittable for two innings. It's unbelievable." In 1999 Wagner, then only 28 years old, averaged almost 15 strikeouts per 9 innings, a marvelous feat.

One-time Tigers pitching coach Dan Warthen felt one of Wagner's keys was "he doesn't look like he's throwing as hard as he's throwing [capable of hitting 100 mph on radar guns]. You use the term 'sneaky' [fast], but how can you say 96 and 97 is sneaky? But it's just easy for him—the great leg drive, very quick arm through the zone, and smooth. He's a little guy [listed at 5′10″ and 180 pounds], but he gets that hand through the zone."

Warthen realizes that some radar guns are generous in their speed estimations but believes Wagner's printouts. In a pitchers' duel versus the Pirates in Pittsburgh, a game eventually won by the Pirates in an extra inning no-hitter, the scoreboard displayed a 101 mph reading on one of Wagner's pitches. Warthen commented, "With everything right and he's feeling fresh, he's got the capability of hitting that velocity."

Wagner said that he was particularly pumped up during that game. "I think tight games have a lot to do with it. I don't think necessarily the hitter [is the key factor]. Once you kinda get established and you've been through it a little bit, you don't really sit there and go, 'Hey, this guy [is tough].' I don't throw any harder against Barry Bonds than I would do against [Jason] Kendall or [Brian] Giles."

With Wagner's stuff, it's little wonder that, in 1999, he recorded more saves than hits allowed (39 to 35), an incredible feat that only superstars Dennis Eckersley, Trevor Hoffman, and Mariano Rivera had ever done before.

Ironically, the modest Wagner doesn't seem to realize that his fastball is so overpowering that hitters wish they didn't have to see it. "I can't imagine," Wagner commented, "somebody fearing me." He admitted he's heard players say they don't like facing him, but he says he's never seen the fear that he is capable of instilling.

John Wetteland

In 1999, Jim Lefebvre cast his "vote" for John Wetteland as the most effective hard-throwing reliever in the game. "He's just a great pitcher," he began. "He goes out there and, 'Here it is, man.' He comes after you hard with his fastball, curveball, slider. If you're going to face him, you're going to have to hit his best stuff." And back then, that best stuff came in at up to 96 mph.

Still, while he was all business once he left the bullpen, another of his "secret" tools was his crazy sense of humor. Infamous for his pranks and practical jokes out in the bullpen, he was able to stay loose despite the rigors and demands of his role.

Early Wynn

Many of the stories of Wynn's feistiness are either exaggerated a bit or wildly embellished. For example, the legend of Wynn saying he would knock down his own mother (or grandmother) is an apocryphal one.

However, Wynn did feel as if the plate belonged to him, so he did drill many a hitter. A minor leaguer who was in the Indians system during the Wynn era was asked if he believed the old tale concerning Wynn being capable of knocking down his grandmother if she crowded the plate. He responded, "I don't think so, because when I knew him I think his grandmother was dead. But," he added, adding to the myth, "his mother was another story."

Wynn supposedly perpetuated the legend: "I'm tired of hearing all those stories that I'd throw at my mother." He paused for effect, then added, "Unless she had a bat in her hand."

Bob Feller said those famous lines, which typified Wynn's attitude, were never uttered by the great competitor. Feller scoffed, "It's kind of like other legends—it's hype." Another line attributed often to Wynn, this one said to be true as well as being typical of his spirit, is: "That space between the white lines—that's my office. That's where I conduct my business."

Another true tale emphasizes Wynn's determination. One spring a Triple-A minor leaguer stepped into the box to face Wynn, who was merely working out some kinks in his back. The young hitter smashed a grounder through the box. He recounted, "It went right through Wynn's legs. In those days they didn't have the screen in front of the pitcher during batting practice.

"I knew what was coming next, so I started to walk away. Wynn called to me, 'Hey, get back in there.'"

At first, the hitter refused, but Wynn insisted and promised he wouldn't seek revenge. Predictably, he was lying, and promptly threw at the kid. Even in a meaningless workout, Wynn simply had to establish who the boss was.

Bibliography

Books

Cairns, Bob. *Pen Men*. New York: St. Martin's Press, 1992.

Connor, Anthony J. *Baseball for the Love of It*. New York: Macmillan, 1982.

Craig, Roger. *Inside Pitch*. Grand Rapids, Mich.: Wm. B. Eerdmans Pub. Co., 1984.

Dickson, Paul. *Baseball's Greatest Quotations*. New York: Harper Perennial, 1991.

Halberstam, David. *Summer of '49*. New York: W. Morrow, 1989.

Hernandez, Keith. *Pure Baseball*. New York: Harper Collins, 1994.

House, Tom. *The Winning Pitcher*. Chicago: Contemporary Books, 1988.

Leonard, Bernardo. *The Superstar Hitter's Bible*. Lincolnwood, Ill.: Contemporary Books, 1998.

Mazzone, Leo. *Pitch Like a Pro*. New York: St. Martin's Griffin, 1999.

Palmer, Jim. *Pitching*. New York: Antheneum, 1975.

Quigley, Martin. *The Crooked Pitch*. Chapel Hill, N.C.: Algonquin Books, 1984.

Ripken Sr., Cal. *The Ripken Way*. New York: Pocket Books, 1999.

Rosen, Ira. *Blue Skies, Green Fields*. New York: Clarkson Potter, 2001.

Ryan, Nolan. *Nolan Ryan's Pitcher's Bible.* New York: Simon & Schuster, 1991.

Stewart, Wayne. *Fathers, Sons & Baseball.* Guilford, Conn.: Lyons Press, 2002.

————. *Indians on the Game.* Cleveland: Gray & Co., 2001.

Thorn, John, and John Holway. *The Pitcher.* New York: Prentice Hall, 1987.

Veeck, Bill, and Ed Linn. *Veeck as in Wreck.* New York: Putnam, 1962.

Periodicals

Associated Press
Baseball Digest
Chop Talk: The Official Monthly Magazine of the Atlanta Braves
Cleveland Plain Dealer
The Morning Journal (Lorain, Ohio)
San Diego Union-Tribune
Sports Illustrated
USA Today/Baseball Weekly
USA Today/Sports Weekly

Index

About the Author

WAYNE STEWART WAS born and raised in Donora, Pennsylvania, a town that has produced several big-league baseball players, including Stan Musial and the father-son Griffeys. He now lives in Lorain, Ohio, with his wife, Nancy (Panich) Stewart. They have two sons, Sean and Scott.

Stewart has covered the baseball world as a writer since 1978. He has interviewed and profiled many Hall of Famers, such as Nolan Ryan, Bob Gibson, Robin Yount, Gaylord Perry, Warren Spahn, and Willie Stargell as well as probable future Hall of Famers Joe Torre, Tony Gwynn, Greg Maddux, Rickey Henderson, Mike Schmidt, Frank Thomas, and Ken Griffey Jr. He has also interviewed and written stories about some of the biggest names in other sports, including Kareem Abdul-Jabbar, Larry Bird, and Jimmy Brown.

He has written seventeen baseball books to date, including *Baseball Oddities, Baseball Bafflers, Baseball Puzzlers, Indians on the Game, Fathers, Sons, and Baseball*, and ten juvenile baseball books featuring the history of ten big-league franchises. His work has also appeared in several baseball anthologies.

In addition, Mr. Stewart has had nearly seven hundred articles published by *Baseball Digest, USA Today/Baseball Weekly, Boys' Life*, and Beckett Publications. He has also written for many major league official publications for teams such as the Braves, Yankees, White Sox, Orioles, Padres, Twins, Phillies, Red Sox, A's, and Dodgers.

Mr. Stewart has appeared as a baseball expert and historian on Cleveland's Fox 8 and on an ESPN Classic documentary of Bob Feller. He has also hosted his own radio shows on a small station in Lorain—a call-in sports talk show, a pregame Indians report, pregame Notre Dame shows, and broadcasts of local baseball contests.